The Simplicity
of Living
by Faith

The Simplicity
of Living
by Faith

David Corbin

Winchester, UK
Washington, USA

First published by Circle Books, 2013
Circle Books is an imprint of John Hunt Publishing Ltd., Laurel House, Station Approach,
Alresford, Hants, SO24 9JH, UK
office1@jhpbooks.net
www.johnhuntpublishing.com
www.circle-books.com

For distributor details and how to order please visit the 'Ordering' section on our website.

Text copyright: David Corbin 2013

ISBN: 978 1 78279 259 8

A CIP catalogue record for this book is available from the British Library.

Design: Stuart Davies

Printed in the USA by Edwards Brothers Malloy

We operate a distinctive and ethical publishing philosophy in all
areas of our business, from our global network of authors to
production and worldwide distribution.

CONTENTS

ACKNOWLEDGEMENTS

I want to thank God, who through the Holy Spirit, inspired me to write this book, and gave me the insight for the common good and the building up of other Believers today, being our final authority in all matters pertaining to doctrine, reproof, correction, and instruction in righteousness (2 Tim. 3:16,17).

I would like to express my gratitude to my father, Rev. Bob van der Berg, who has shared his wealth of knowledge gained from serving the Lord in ministry, and who reviewed this book to confirm that I have understood the prompting of the Holy Spirit correctly in proclaiming the truth of the Gospel, as well as offered assistance and support.

Also, I would also like to thank my wife, Letitia Corbin, for her support and continuous encouragement whilst researching and writing this book, as well as her commitment to me in understanding the precepts of God's Word.

David J. Corbin

Introduction

Faith plays a role in our everyday lives more than we might think. As Christians, we all have faith to some degree. The Bible says in Rom. 12:3 that each of us is given "...the measure of faith" (KJV). You trust that the chair you are about to sit on will hold you and that the lights will come on when you flip the switch....

Yet there is much confusion about faith today just as there has always been. It is easy to have faith in the little things, as many Christians exercise their faith by what they can see, hear and or feel. But what about when it comes to trusting God? Do you struggle to apply that same kind of faith in Him? Someday that chair may eventually break and the electricity may go out, but God is the only one who will never fail you. Everything the LORD does for us is accessed through faith. The Bible is our manual with detailed teachings and instructions about faith; but just like in the natural, few people take the time to really study the manual. They are impatient and want to do it on their own. They may reach some level of success, but to really be proficient, they have to read the manual.

Faith is based on knowledge, and everything we need to know to be a victorious Christian is explained in God's Word. This book will provide you with the knowledge of a few basic truths and fundamentals about faith that when properly understood and applied, will set in motion the releasing of His power and your ability to change your circumstances and move those mountains in your life.

My prayer is that as you read this book, the Word of God will become a reality in your heart, and the Holy Spirit will give you knowledge of His will in all wisdom and spiritual understanding, that you may walk worthy of the LORD as your spirit becomes alive to His Word, fully pleasing Him, being fruitful in every good work and increasing in the knowledge of God.

This book is not copyright protected, as the content is God-inspired. Therefore, use this book, or portions thereof, and distribute it to equip like-minded men and women; teaching spiritual truths, imparting biblical knowledge, and grounding them in the message of God's unconditional love and grace.

Chapter 1

What is Faith?

1.1 Introduction

Few words are more central to the Christian message, or more often used to describe Christian experience than faith. Yet this word is often corrupted by a misunderstanding of its biblical meaning. Many Christians today use the word 'faith' to indicate what is possible but uncertain. However, the Bible depicts faith in ways that links it to what is assuredly and certainly true. Faith is being used today, just as it has been in the past, in a subjective manner; meaning our act of faith, or strength of faith, is the outcome of what was acquired or achieved through effort. But the Bible shifts our attention from a subjective experience and centres it on the objective of our faith – God Himself and our personal relationship with Him in Jesus Christ!

1.2 Old Testament concept of faith

The closest Hebrew parallel to the New Testament word for 'faith' is *ăman* (Strong's Expanded Exhaustive Concordance, Hebrew and Aramaic Dictionary Number: 540). The root of this word indicates firmness and certainty. This Old Testament term captures the biblical meaning of faith, and expresses a concrete conviction based on the reliability of what is believed. Other aspects of this faith relationship with God are expressed in the following Hebrew words: *Bātah* and *Mahseh*. Both these words express the idea of trust in, or reliance on another. The Old Testament concept of faith as firmness and certainty is ingrained in the view of God as applicable to the Old Testament. This is confirmed through Psa. 26:1 where the Psalmist writes "Vindicate me, O Lord, for I have walked in my integrity. I have also trusted in the Lord; I shall not slip". In this scripture the

3

Psalmist does appeal to his integrity, but that is not an indication of his trusting himself or his deeds. His trust is in God, and his integrity is the evidence of that trust. Using Abraham and Israel as two examples of how faith operated in the Old Testament, it is evident that Abraham is a biblical illustration of faith as a believing response to God, and his faith was demonstrated as he subsequently acted on what God had said (Gen. 12 – 22). Abraham took the LORD at His word, and his whole outlook was changed. Abraham's life was transformed as he translated faith into obedience (Jas. 2:22). For Israel however, a generation experienced many miraculous events, all providing unmistakeable evidence of God's reality and power, but their unbelieving hearts kept them from experiencing the promises of God due to their disobedience and distrust (Heb. 3:12-19). Psa. 78 speaks of God being angry because the Exodus generation would "...not believe in God, and did not trust in His salvation... and did not believe in His wondrous works" (Psa. 78:22-32). They refused to take God into account when they faced a formidable foe in Canaan, and their lack of faith was translated into disobedience. As a result, that generation died in the wilderness.

The Old Testament saints were required to adhere to the Old Covenant (Mosaic Law), and we read little of faith under the Mosaic Law as the focus of the Old Testament was on the covenant God established with Israel, and faith was expressed through obedience to the keeping of the commandments and decrees that governed Israel, of which there were 613 commandments. Every Old Testament saint faced a choice between belief and unbelief. God spoke to every generation anew, in the Law and through prophets. Those who believed and placed their trust in God demonstrated their faith just as Abraham had done, by obedience to the Word of promise, and they were blessed. Those who disbelieved disregarded the written and prophetic Word and experienced God's judgement. In the Old Testament then, faith was essentially a response to God. It was about the individuals' inner conviction and commitment to God, translated into action, and that resulted in a lifestyle through which the reality of faith was expressed. A study of the Old Testament reveals that there was a requirement for a right attitude towards God; in other words, faith: "Trust in the Lord, and do good... Delight yourself also in the Lord, and He shall give you the desires of your heart. Commit your way to the Lord, trust also in Him, and He shall bring it to pass" (Psa. 37:3-5). There is no doubt that the Psalmist was advocating a good attitude; calling on men to put their trust in the LORD, which is another way of telling them to live by faith. The Old Testament saints were urged to put their faith in God (Pro. 3:5).

1.3 The New Testament concept of faith

The New Testament word for 'faith' in the Greek is *pistis* (Strong's Expanded Exhaustive Concordance, Greek Dictionary Number: 4102). The word group attached to *pistis* encompasses a wide range of secular and religious ideas, but the underlying root for this word indicates relationships established by trust and maintained by trustworthiness. The *pistis* word group used in the New Testament depicts a person committing himself/herself totally to Jesus Christ, for our faith is into Jesus (Eph. 1:15; Col. 1:4; 2 Tim. 3:15). In John 14:6 we read Jesus saying "...I am the way, the truth, and the life. No one comes to the Father except through Me". God revealed Himself through Jesus, and set Jesus before us as the One to whom we must entrust ourselves for salvation. For that reason there are not many scriptures in the New Testament that have God as the object of faith (John 12:44; John 14:1; Acts 16:34; Rom. 4:3, 5, 17, 24; Gal. 3:6; 1 Thes. 1:8; Tit. 3:8; Heb. 6:1; 1 Pet. 1:21). Jesus is now the focus of Christian faith. Therefore, the New Testament concept of faith relates to our relationship with Jesus, and refers to (a) the trust that a Christian places in the Son of Man and (b), the dedication to Him that grows out of that very personal commitment.

Even though Israel saw Jesus heal the sick amongst them, cast out demons, and even witnessed Him raise Lazarus from the dead, these miracles failed to produce true faith. They rejected Jesus against the evidence of the Lord's indisputable miracles they saw and experienced (John 10:38; John 14:11). This is similar to Israel's unbelieving hearts amid the unarguable miracles they saw and experienced that proved God's power and presence whilst they were in the wilderness. But Jesus made it clear in Matt. 21:22 when He said "And whatever things you ask in prayer, believing, you will receive" that a lack of trust in God obstructs life's possibilities. When we fail to believe, we do not experience the promises of God. In contrast, when we do believe, we allow God to use His power in and through us (Matt.17:20; Matt. 21:21; Luke 7:9-10). All things are possible to them that believe. For Christians today, faith in Jesus does not come through the observation of miracles. Faith is intuitive as we learn about Jesus, study and understand what He said, take Him at His word, and put our trust in Him. From trust, we mature our faith to an active reliance on the power and presence of God, and experience God at work in our lives! Faith does not reside within a doctrine, but rather in a person and the trustworthiness of that person (Heb. 11:6).

1.4 Now faith is

I am certain that you have heard Heb. 11:1 "Now faith is the substance of things hoped for, the evidence of things not seen" mentioned or quoted. But have you ever considered what this verse means? Is faith the substance or the evidence? From Scripture we see that there are two kinds of faith – the Thomas-like faith (or head faith), and the Abraham-like faith (or heart faith). The Thomas-like faith is limited to our five physical senses. Everyone, both believer and unbeliever, has this kind of faith. We use this kind of faith when we board an aeroplane despite not fully understanding how flying works, or assessing the pilot's credentials, but we trust that the flight will be okay. However, the Abraham-like faith is the same supernatural faith we use to receive salvation. There is a big difference between believing with your heart and believing what your five senses tell you! In Heb. 11:1 the writer of Hebrews is talking about this supernatural faith: the God-kind of faith or the Abraham-kind of faith; and every believer has the measure of this kind of faith.

Reading the scripture again "...faith is the substance of things hoped for..." suggests that hope does not have any substance of itself; for if it did, it would not need faith to give it substance. The verse says that "...faith is the **substance**..." of things hoped for, indicating that whatever we hope for, as long as we have our hopes in a type of **hoping** stage, our hope will remain in that state – having no essence. To illustrate it in another way: hope is like dreaming. Have you ever had a dream where you were in a competition, and you had won. You were about to receive your prize when a noise awoke you. You quickly closed your eyes and tried to carry on with your dream where you left off, but the dream was gone.... The dream was gone because it had no substance. Dreams have no tangibility, no materiality and no substance; and that is similar to the way hope is unless faith is added to it. When faith is added to hope, it gains tangibility, materiality and substance. For this reason we need to understand what is meant by substance. This word 'substance' in the Greek is *hupŏstasis* (Strong's Expanded Exhaustive Concordance, Greek Dictionary Number: 5287), and it means confident or confidence. Looking at the definition of substance in a dictionary denotes that of which a thing consists, physical matter or material. Consequently, we can say that substance is something that can be perceived by our physical senses. It is something that we can see, hear, taste, smell and feel. As a result, we can rephrase Heb. 11:1 to read as follows: "Faith is the physical matter or material anticipated with confidence...". Faith is the action of applying tangibility or materiality to hope in order to bring that which is being hoped for into reality. If we liken faith to money, we can say that it is the money that makes our expectation for something materialise or happen as we pay for and buy what we were hoping for.

Then, to understand what is meant by 'evidence'; the word in the Greek is *ĕlĕgchŏs* (Strong's Expanded Exhaustive Concordance, Greek Dictionary Number: 1650), and it means proof and conviction. Hence, evidence or proof is that which substantiates, validates, or proves the existence of something that was not obvious at a certain point in time. Evidence is a fact or situation that suggests something might be true. For example, your jacket in my car is evidence that you were in my car. Continuing to read the verse "...faith is the... **evidence** of things not seen", we can see that faith is the evidence or the proof, not our physical bodies, not our circumstances, but faith is the evidence. That means that faith takes the place of whatever it is the evidence of, or what we believe for, until that evidence or what we believe for materialises or happens. Therefore, for any given instance, faith is temporary for that given instance until that instance materialises or happens. Once we have the evidence of what we were believing for, we no longer need any evidence.

There is another word in Heb. 11:1 that is very important. Reading the verse again "...faith is ... of things not **seen**". What do you think of when you hear the word see or seen. Of course, eyes immediately come to mind. However, in this verse it is not referring to seeing with your physical eyes; and this is where many Christians have missed the concept of faith and have become confused concerning faith, because they have been trying to see faith with their physical eyes. Our eyes form part of our central nervous system which takes information from the retina as electrical signals and delivers it to the brain where this information is interpreted as a visual image of the world around us. If this verse was referring to our physical eyes, then it is implying that we are to use our physical senses to exercise our faith by what they can see, hear and or feel. However, there are some things that we can see but cannot hear, things that we can hear but we cannot touch, things we can feel but we cannot smell, and things we can smell but we cannot taste. Therefore, in this verse the writer of Hebrews is referring to our sensory perception as opposed to physical eyes. That encompasses everything our body uses to acquire information to build a representation of our surrounding world. For example, if your ankle was hurting, what was it that made you think that there was something wrong with your ankle? It could be that your ankle was sore to the touch, swollen, discoloured, or inflexible. Your physical senses told you that there was something wrong with your ankle. Therefore, our knowledge of the outside world depends on our modes of perception, and for that reason this verse is referring to our sensory awareness as opposed to our perception of the eye only.

Taking the above into consideration, we can rephrase Heb. 11:1 to now read as follows: "Faith is the physical matter or material anticipated with confidence, the evidence or proof of things not perceived by our physical senses". Faith is hearing the inaudible, seeing the invisible, and doing the impossible!

1.5 What is faith to you?

I believe that what God is telling us in Heb.11:1 is that faith is laying hold of the unseen area of hope and bringing it into the area of reality. Too many times when it comes to receiving the Holy Spirit, healing, or an answer to prayer, many Christians simply hope they will receive. But it is not hoping that gets the job done; it is believing. If you have said 'I trust God heard my prayer', that is not faith, that is hope; because hope is always future tense or pointing to the future. The Bible says, "Now faith is...". If it is not now, it is not faith. It is also unscriptural to pray 'if it be Your will...' concerning anything God has already promised us in His Word. When you begin a prayer with 'if', you are in doubt. Christians are of the opinion that they are being humble when they pray that way; but that is ignorance, especially when God has revealed His will to us through the Bible. It is only when you are praying a prayer of consecration that you place an 'if' in the prayer; for example, when you believe God wants you to move to another city or start a new job and you are not certain, then you ask God that His will be done or that He show you what His will is. That is a prayer of consecration. A faith statement says 'I will receive right now; I believe I have my petition now as I pray' (Mark 11:24). Many Christians read what God's Word says and acknowledge that as being true, but they acknowledge with their minds only. Faith is not of the mind or the body, it is of the heart. It is with heart-faith that we receive from God. The Bible reaffirms this in Rom. 10.10 where it says "For with the **heart** one believes..." (emphasis mine). Similarly, Mark 11:23 says "...whoever says... and does not doubt in his **heart**..." (emphasis mine). In Pro. 3:5 it says "Trust in the Lord with all your **heart**, and lean not on your own understanding" (emphasis mine). You must understand that the word 'heart' as used in these scriptures does not refer to the muscular organ that pumps blood to your body; for if it did, these scriptures would indicate that you can believe with your physical body, which does not make sense as you can no more believe God with your physical heart than you can believe Him with your physical hand or foot!

The terms 'spirit of man' and 'heart of man' are used interchangeably throughout the Bible. But to understand what the Bible describes as the heart of man, look at 1 Pet. 3:4 where it says "...rather let it be the **hidden person of the heart**, with the incorruptible beauty of a gentle and quiet spirit..." (emphasis mine). This hidden person of the heart in this verse is describing the inward man, or the spirit of man; hence implying that the spirit comprises only a part of the heart. The heart of man is actually made up of two parts: the soul and the spirit. This is the reason the scripture speaks of having two minds in our hearts (Jas. 4:8) and why we must believe with all our hearts (Acts 8:37), and not just a part. The inward man is hidden from our human sensory organs as it is not a physical being. In 2 Cor. 4:16 Paul made mention of this inward man when he said "Therefore we do not lose heart. Even though our outward man is perishing, yet the inward man is being renewed day by day". Paul mentioned that there is both an outward and an inward man. We can physically behold the outward man, which is our body; but we cannot see and feel the inward man as it is spirit. God's Word clearly teaches that we are three-part beings, but very few Christians have a functional understanding of spirit, soul, and body. In Dan. 7:15 it is written, "I, Daniel, was grieved in my **spirit** within my **body**, and the visions of my **head** (soul) troubled me" (emphasis mine). This pronounces that man is a spirit being, made in the image and likeness of God (Gen. 1:27). It is not in our physical bodies that we are like God, for the Bible says that God is not a man (John 4:24). Man has a soul (namely a personality, being the mind, the will, the emotions, and the conscience), and lives in a body. Paul reaffirms this statement by writing in 1 Thes. 5: 23 "Now may the God of peace Himself sanctify you completely; and may your whole **spirit** (*pnĕuma*), **soul** (*psuchē*) and **body** (*sōma*) be preserved blameless at the coming of our Lord Jesus Christ" (emphasis mine). Your body is obvious and needs no further explanation. However, from the aforementioned scriptures and explanation there is a distinct difference between your spirit and soul. Some Christians mistakenly think that the mind/head (soul) is the spirit; but the mind is not the spirit. Matt. 6:13 confirms that our soul and body have been purchased by Jesus' blood, and our born-again spirits have been eternally redeemed (Heb. 9:12). Heb. 4:12 describes the Word of God as being "...sharper than any two-edged sword, piercing even to the division of soul and spirit...". In his letter to the Romans, Paul asserts that the spirit is in the heart of man when he says "For he is not a Jew who is one outwardly, nor is circumcision that which is outward in the flesh; but he is a Jew who is one inwardly; and circumcision is that **of the heart, in the Spirit**, not in the letter; whose praise is not from men but from God" (Rom. 2:28-19) (emphasis mine). This has led some Christians to believe that the soul and spirit are the same. 1 Cor. 14:14 says "For if I pray in a tongue, my spirit prays, but my **understanding** (mind) is unfruitful" (emphasis mine). This scripture indicates that when we speak in tongues, it does not come from our mind, or out of our own human thinking, but from our spirit, from our innermost being, from the Holy Spirit within our spirit.

If you were physically in the same room with me and talking to me, you would be able to see me in my physical body, but you would be speaking to my soul. You can feel both your body and your soul, and they are receiving and transmitting information all the time. For example, if I asked you if you were either hungry or thirsty, you would not have to pray about it and get back to me. You instantly know whether you are either hungry or thirsty. Likewise, if I asked how you felt emotionally, you will not have to ponder your emotions and tell me later. You will know whether you are cheerful, miserable, relieved or angry at any moment. It is easy to know how your body feels, what is going on in your mind, and what emotions you are experiencing. However, your spirit is different; it cannot be accessed through your five physical senses. John 3:6 says "That which is born of the flesh is flesh, and that which is born of the Spirit is spirit". Jesus was emphasising that there is no direct connection between the two. They are interrelated, but spirit is spirit and flesh is flesh. You simply cannot contact your spirit through your emotions or your physical body. Therefore, where the Bible refers to the heart, it is referring to the inward man, or spirit of man; and not the physical organ that pumps blood to your body.

1.6 Believing with the heart

To believe with the heart means to believe with the spirit. To believe with the heart means to believe apart from what your physical body or your five senses may tell you. Both the physical body and five senses believe according to what can be perceived in the natural. Even if you have doubt in your head, faith will still work in your heart. 'Doubt' in the Greek is *diakrinō* (Strong's Expanded Exhaustive Concordance, Greek Dictionary Number: 1252), and suggests uncertainty about something set as an object of faith. In Rom. 4:13-21 Paul refers to Abraham and describes the patriarch as being fully aware of his own advanced age and of Sarah having gone far beyond menopause. Yet God appears to them and promises Abraham that he will father a multitude. Paul says of Abraham "And not being weak in faith, he did not consider his own body, already dead (since he was about a hundred years old), and the deadness of Sarah's womb. He did not waver at the promise of God through unbelief... being fully convinced that what He had promised He was also able to perform" (Rom. 4:19-21).

No one is immune to doubt, it affects us all. The secret, however, is to know how to handle doubt when it arises. Even the greatest men and women of God recorded in the Bible had to deal with doubt. Jesus said of John the Baptist: "Assuredly, I say to you, among those born of women there has not risen one greater than John the Baptist" (Matt. 11:11). That means, for Jesus, John was greater than Abraham, Joseph, Moses, David, or any other Old Testament saint you can name. Yet John doubted the most important thing of all by questioning whether Jesus was really the Christ. John the Baptist had been thrown into prison for criticising Herod on marrying his brother's wife, an incestuous relationship. While in prison he became so discouraged that he asked two of his disciples to go to Jesus and ask Him if He really was the Christ. When you consider who John the Baptist was, he was separated and focused on his purpose. His entire life was committed to preparing the way for the Messiah. He spent thirty years preparing for a ministry that only lasted six months. John saw Jesus and said "...Behold! The Lamb of God who takes away the sin of the world!" (John 1:29). When John baptised Jesus in the Jordan River, he saw the Spirit of God, shaped as a dove, descend from heaven and come to rest on the Messiah. At that moment, John was absolutely certain that Jesus was the Christ. God had revealed to him that through a visible sign from heaven he would know who the Christ was. For that reason, he said "And I have seen and testified that this is the Son of God" (John 1:34). However, after being imprisoned for a period of time, he began to doubt. What strikes me as amazing is how Jesus responded to John's doubt.... He told John's disciples to go back and tell him of the miracles they had witnessed and that John would be blessed if he would just believe. That is all He said! Jesus neither empathised with John nor made any complimentary remarks. Jesus reserved such comments until after John's disciples had left (Luke 7:24-28). I heard another minister mention this, and elaborate that a kind or sympathetic word would have been more helpful for John than telling him of the miracles being performed. Reading Matthew's account of this (Matt. 11:4-6) we see that Jesus performed all the miracles as prophesied by Isaiah (Isa. 35:5-6), thereby fulfilling the prophecy about Himself; and for that reason Jesus did not attempt to make John feel better with a few kind words, or an emotional touch, and it was not because He did not care about John; on the contrary, He cared for John so much that He gave John His best, the written Word of God. Jesus reminded John of the Scriptures, to deal with his doubts. This is how Jesus dealt with His own temptations (Matt. 4); and similarly, this is how Jesus deals with our doubts. Many of us have a Bible or two. Some lay around gathering dust and some accompany us wherever we go. But when unbelief afflicts us, we usually want something emotional that we can feel, rather than a scripture. We would rather have

Jesus put His arms around us and tell how everything will be all right. But overcoming doubt is not just about feeling better; it is about getting back into faith that only comes from the Word of God (Rom. 10:17). Smith Wigglesworth once said, 'I cannot understand God by feelings. I cannot understand the Lord Jesus Christ by feelings. I can understand God the Father and Jesus Christ only by what the Word says about them. God is everything the Word says He is'. Too many Christians are trying to get acquainted with God through feelings, and when they feel good, they think God has heard them. But if they do not feel good, they think He is not hearing them. Their faith is based on their feelings, rather than being based on God's Word. If God's Word says He hears you, then you must know He hears you because He said so, and His Word cannot lie. Therefore, if your faith is based on feelings, then you are using natural human faith. Attempting to get spiritual results using natural human faith will not work.

Jesus sent the Word back with John's disciples. He knew that would inspire John's spirit to overcome the doubt. Peter understood this about faith when he wrote in 2 Pet. 1:12-15 "For this reason I will not be negligent to remind you always of these things, though you know and are established in the present truth. Yes, I think it is right, as long as I am in this tent, to stir you up by reminding you, knowing that shortly I must put off my tent, just as our Lord Jesus Christ showed me. Moreover I will be careful to ensure that you always have a reminder of these things after my decease". Peter was reminding the Believers in Asia Minor of the eternal consequences of this truth, being the Word of God (1 Thes. 2:13). In the following verses, to prove to them that his eyewitness of Christ Jesus and His transfiguration are distinct from the stories of the heathen priests and their gods, Peter refers to the time James, John and he were with Jesus on the mountain, and they saw Jesus shine as the brightness of the sun. The glory of the LORD as a cloud overshadowed them all, and they heard an audible voice out of heaven say "This is My beloved Son. Hear Him!" (Mark 9:7). They even witnessed Moses and Elijah talking with Jesus. But Peter went on to say in 2 Pet. 1:19, "And so we have the prophetic word confirmed...". What could possibly be more certain than all these supernatural signs? Peter records in 2 Pet. 1:20 that the Scriptures are more certain, more faith building and doubt destroying than seeing Jesus transfigured or hearing an audible voice from heaven! Placing your faith in the Word of God and depending on this absolutely certain Word of prophecy is the only sure way to overcome doubt. Do not allow your thoughts to be dominated by your five physical senses. You need to come to a place where God's Word is more real to you than anything you can see, hear, taste, smell, or feel. When in doubt, refer to the Word of God in the same way that Jesus pointed John the Baptist back to the Word of God. Faith comes by hearing and hearing by the Word (Rom. 10:17). We need only to realise that whatever our circumstances, the overriding fact is the reality of God. Jesus never said that we should not doubt in our mind. Pro. 3:5 repeats this by saying "Trust in the Lord with all your heart, and lean not on your own under-standing". Faith is not about our human emotions and physical senses; it is about what God's Word says that is important. Jesus said in Matt. 4:4 "...man shall not live by bread alone, but by every word that proceeds from the mouth of God". The Word of God is to the spirit of man what natural food is to the body of man.

1.7 Faith is substance

Many Christians think faith is acting like something has happened when in reality it has not, and if we imagine this for long enough, then it will come to pass. But that is not what faith is. Looking again at Heb. 11:1, the verse does not say "...things that do not exist...". They do exist, but are not visible in the natural realm. It is the evidence of things not seen. In the natural realm there are things that do exist that are not visible. We cannot see radio waves, but we know they exist when we place our food in the microwave oven and switch the oven on. By warming the food, the microwave oven has not made unseen radio waves visible. When we see the steam, it is not when those radio waves became real. They were already there. A microwave oven does not generate radio waves, but passes microwave radiation through the food, thereby causing the food to heat. But I am sure that you have experienced an occasion when you switched the microwave oven on and nothing happened. I am certain that the first thing you did was neither telephone the microwave manufacturer and complain that the microwave was no longer passing microwave radiation through your food, nor was it to telephone your energy provider and complain that they had removed you from the national grid; but rather it was to check and confirm that everything was working on your microwave oven. Specifically, you would have confirmed that the electricity was on, that the microwave oven was plugged into the wall socket, and that the distribution board in your house had not tripped. What I am implying is that you checked your microwave oven to see what was wrong with it. You trusted that the microwave manufacturer produced a reliable oven, and that your energy provider had not stopped providing electricity. You would not question that until you had eliminated all the possible problems with your microwave oven. Likewise, God is real and does exist. He just cannot be seen. When the LORD created the universe, Gen. 1:3 tells us that He created light on the first day but did not create the sun, moon, and stars until the fourth day of creation (Gen. 1:14-19). The Lord called light into being first and four days later created a source for the light to come from. That is not the way natural man does things. We are limited, but God calls things that are not as though they were. We assume that because we have not experienced the victory in our lives that Jesus provided, nothing has happened. That is incorrect. We need to have more faith in God than we have in mankind and the natural realm. Another good illustration in the Bible of this is in 2 Kgs. 6. Elisha, the prophet of God, was revealing the Syrians' battle plans to the king of Israel. Every time the king of Syria tried to ambush the king of Israel, Elisha would warn the king of Israel, and he would counter the Syrians' ambush. This happened so often that the king of Syria finally concluded that there had to be a traitor in his presence. He knew that the king of Israel could not be operating without inside information. When one of the servants to the king of Syria said that Elisha was revealing the words that the king of Syria spoke in his bed chamber to the king of Israel, the king of Syria sent his armies to capture Elisha. 2 Kgs. 6:15 records this event: "And when the servant of the man of God arose early and went out, there was an army, surrounding the city with horses and chariots. And his servant said to him, 'Alas, my master! What shall we do?'" (I have heard another minister say this was old English for 'he panicked'). Elisha knew why the Syrian army had come. Look at Elisha's comment to this situation in verse 16: "...Do not fear, for those who are with us are more than those who are with them".

People who do not believe anything exists beyond their five physical senses would say Elisha was lying. He was confessing that something was a certain way when in reality it was not, hoping that it would become so. But Elisha was speaking the truth. There were more with him than there was with the Syrian army. The fact is that Elisha's help was in the unseen realm. The key to understanding this illustration is to recognise that there is another realm of reality beyond this physical world. Those who are limited to only their five physical senses will always struggle with this. In the physical world you could count the Syrian soldiers by the thousands, and there was only Elisha and his servant. But in the spiritual realm, there were many more horses and chariots of fire around Elisha than there were Syrian soldiers. We read on in 2 Kgs. 6:17, and the scripture says, "And Elisha prayed, and said, 'Lord, I pray, open his eyes that he may see'. Then the Lord opened the eyes of the young man, and he saw. And behold, the mountain was full of horses and chariots of fire all around Elisha". You can be assured that Gehazi's physical eyes were already wide open, but God now opened his spiritual eyes. He was able to see with his heart (being his spirit) into the spiritual world. And when the spiritual world was taken into consideration, then Elisha's statement was perfectly true.

Those who see faith as an attempt to make something real which is not real will always struggle with those who see faith as simply making what is spiritually true a physical truth. Those who limit truth to only the physical realm would have called Elisha a 'name it, claim it, blab it, and grab it' cultist. But by saying that, they condemn themselves, and show they only consider what they can see, taste, hear, smell, and feel to be reality. Such people are what the Bible calls 'carnal' (Rom. 8:6-7). When Gehazi's spiritual eyes were opened, the Syrian army did not disappear. They were still there. The physical reality was still true, but there was a greater spiritual truth that emerged. True faith does not deny physical truth, but refuses to let physical truth dominate spiritual truth. True faith subdues physical truth to the reality of spiritual truth. Because Elisha believed in the realities of the spiritual world, he raised his hand and struck the Syrian army with blindness. Then he led the whole Syrian army captive to the king of Israel! The Bible gives no indication that Elisha saw the horses and chariots of fire around him; but he did not need to see. He knew what was real in the spiritual world, and he controlled his emotions and actions accordingly. Those who operate in true faith do not need to see with their physical eyes; their faith is evidence enough. Faith must be based on the Word of God. Heart faith believes the Word of God; and to believe with the heart means to believe with your spirit, or inward man, which is independent of your head and body. You must receive the revelation of God's Word in your heart. That is why we, as Christians, have to rely on the Holy Spirit to open and unveil the Word to us because the Word of God is of the Spirit, and it is foolish to the natural mind (1 Cor. 2:14).

1.8 Faith and belief

Another matter causing much confusion about faith today is the difference between 'faith' and 'belief'. Although spelt and pronounced differently, in the minds of many Christians these two words mean the same thing, and therefore are interchanged to explain the same thing. As I mentioned above, the New Testament word for 'faith' in the Greek is *pistis* (Strong's Expanded Exhaustive Concordance, Greek Dictionary Number: 4102), and the word 'belief' in the Greek is *pistikos* (Strong's Expanded Exhaustive Concordance, Greek Dictionary Number: 4101). *Pistikos* means genuine, pure, and trustworthy; but has its origin from the word *pistis*. The word *pistis* even has 'belief' as one of its definitions. Consequently, the misunderstanding for most Christians regarding the similarity of faith and belief is understandable as these words are virtually the same, and therefore thought of as two different ways of saying the same thing.

Using an illustration, I will demonstrate that these two words are as different as night is to day, as male is to female; as rich is to poor, and have dissimilar meanings; and hence the need to differentiate between these words. When I say woman, female, lady, wife, or mother, you do not create a mental image of a dog! Although these nouns basically mean the same thing, there are differences if we consider their particular definitions. However, when I use either of these words, you mentally imagine a female human. Likewise, the words faith and belief have come to have the same connotations, though they are different. If you do not understand the difference between faith and belief, you may think you are operating in faith, when in fact you are only operating in belief; and believing will not have any impact on your circumstances. Though you believe, and what you are believing is absolutely, positively, unequivocally, and biblically true, you can still die from sickness and disease and live in poverty although believing. Even though there is a distinct difference between faith and belief, the two are inseparable. Similar to a coin which has a coat of arms on one side and an image on the other side, and both sides need to be intact for the coin to be considered as legal tender, so the Word of God has many sides, representing the various ways of saying the same thing, and these sides need to be intact and brought together for a more accurate and complete understanding of what the Word of God says regarding a particular subject.

Let us imagine that you are walking down the street and stumble across a homeless person laying on the ground in a foetal position, and as he sees you walking by, cries out for help. As you approach him you notice that he seems withered and half-starved. Just then, another stranger comes to his aide and claims to be a medical doctor. The homeless man states that he has not eaten anything for a long time and his movements have now become painful. The doctor examines the homeless man, looks at you and pronounces that this homeless man is malnourished, and the pain is due to muscle atrophy. The doctor then concludes that due to the homeless man's weakened body, brought on through starvation, he only has approximately 30 minutes to live unless he receives some urgent nourishment. To avoid this death, you run to a nearby fast-food outlet and purchase several meals for the homeless man. You place these calorie rich meals beside him and the doctor asks him, 'Sir, do you see this food beside you?' The homeless man acknowledges by nodding his head. The doctor then asks, 'Sir, do you believe that if you eat this food, it will prevent you from starving to death?' With indignation written across his face, the homeless man looks at you and the doctor and says, 'Do you think I am dim-witted; of course I believe that if and when I eat this food it will keep me from starving to death. I absolutely, categorically believe that if and when I eat this food, it will keep me from starving to death'. This conversation continues for another 30 minutes and suddenly the homeless man slumps over! The doctor rushes to him, examines him, and with a grim expression on his face, declares the homeless man dead. Based on what you have read, I am certain that you are of the opinion that what the man believed was true... or was it not true as he did die? This same scenario plays off in the minds of many Christians when they think about preservation, healing, wholeness and prosperity as forming part of our inheritance as children of God. Human reason states that if it is God's will for every Christian to be healed then they would all be healed. But because we see and know of so many Christians that are in poor health and living in poverty, it cannot be God's will to heal everyone and see them prosper. Returning to my illustration of the homeless man, every-thing that the homeless man believed and said was completely and absolutely true, and yet he starved to death whilst confessing and believing, and being surrounded by several calorie rich fast-food meals; and he died because he did not eat the food!

That is the difference between faith and belief. Believing is doing exactly what the homeless man did, but faith is acting on that which you believe. You can believe, but if you do not eat the food, you will still die. You can believe in healing and die of a sore finger; you can believe in prosperity and still live well below the poverty line. You have to act on what you believe. Believing that eating will keep you from starving will not keep you from starving. Eating is the action based on what you believe. It is not enough to believe God's Word on divine healing; you have to act on it as well. You must believe it with your heart, say it with your mouth, and then act it out physically to the extent that you can. Faith is acting on what you believe. This is similar to you getting home from work, taking the keys to your front door out of your pocket or bag, standing in front of the door and saying in an audible voice, 'I believe that these are the keys to my front door. I believe that I can take these keys, open this door and enter my home. I believe that if and when I open the front door and enter, I will be in from the cold'. The reality is that you will stand in front of that door until Jesus comes, and nothing will happen. Why? Nothing will happen until you act on what you believe and place the front door key into the lock, turn it, open the door, and enter your home. Yet everything you proclaimed was undeniably true. It is your home, those are your keys, you can open the door, but you will not unless you act on what you believe. It is not enough just to believe.

Chapter 2

How to Increase Faith

2.1 Introduction

God has stated that without faith it is impossible to please Him (Heb. 11:6), and if it is unachievable for us to have faith, then we have a right to challenge His fairness. But God has told us how to get faith. Therefore, if we do not have faith, we are to blame, and not God. He has provided us with the means whereby faith can be produced, and the responsibility rests with us whether or not we have faith. To blame God for our lack of faith is nothing but ignorance. Only twice in the Bible is it recorded that Jesus marvelled at something. Once He marvelled at the people's great unbelief (Mark 6:6), and in Matt. 8:10 He marvelled at a Gentile soldier's great faith. A faith that made Jesus marvel is worth examining. The centurion had a faith that was in God's Word alone. He did not require Jesus to come to his house and heal his sick servant. If Jesus would just speak the Word, that was all he needed. God's Word is as alive today as it was in the beginning. His Word is health to all of our flesh, and life to them that find it. He sent His Word to heal and deliver us from destruction and more. And for those of us who will place His Word in our hearts and allow that seed to conceive, we will see the manifestation of what we believe and speak. Jesus said in John 5:39 that "...the Scriptures... testify of Me".

2.2 Knowledge equals faith

Knowledge of the truth in God's Word brings faith. The new age movement believes that people can 'believe things into existence', which is not the same kind of faith that Christians should have. Our faith is based on the truth in God's Word. Rom. 10:8 says "...The word is near you, in your mouth and in your heart (that is, the word of faith which we preach)". God's Word is called the word of faith, because His Word builds faith. Therefore, knowing what God's Word has to say about something gives us the ability to believe it. In Mark 9:23 Jesus was telling His disciples, "...If you can believe, all things are possible to him who believes". In this verse, the word 'believes' in the Greek means to trust, to rely on, have confidence in, and to adhere to (Strong's Expanded Exhaustive Concordance, Greek Dictionary Number: 4100). Jesus was in essence telling His disciples that all things (referring to the promises of God) are possible for them who will trust God for them (believe). You cannot believe something that nobody has told you; that is why it is important to know what the Word of God has to say, so that you can believe it. Our faith should be based on God's Word. Rom. 10:17 says "So then faith comes by hearing, and hearing by the word of God". When you look at the original Greek word for 'God' in this scripture, you will notice that it is not *Theos*, but rather *Christos* for Christ. Faith comes by hearing, and hearing the Word of Christ. Also, the word for 'word' in the original Greek has two different meanings. The one is *logos* and the other is *rhema*. The world was created by the *logos* of God. *Logos* is the Word of God as recorded in the Bible, which conveys both directly and indirectly the Word, Jesus Christ (John 1:1). *Logos* will give you all the knowledge about God and His promises, but it will not produce faith. Reading the Bible will contribute to your knowledge and understanding of God, but it will not automatically result in you experiencing a victorious Christian lifestyle. Therefore, in Rom. 10:17 'Word' is not defined as *logos*, but rather *rhema*. Faith comes when you hear the *rhema* Word, being the spoken word of God, and not by simply hearing the Word of God, because the Word of God includes everything in the Bible, including the Old Covenant (Mosaic Law). There is no conveying of faith when you hear the Ten Commandments taught. Faith only comes by hearing the Word of Christ. *Rhema* is a specific word spoken to a specific person in a specific situation.

When Jesus told Peter to come to Him (Matt. 14:29), it was *rhema* not *logos*. Peter received a specific word for a specific situation! *Rhema* brings faith, and faith comes by hearing *rhema*. Peter never walked on water by having a knowledge of God, Peter had a *rhema*. This does not mean however that you should listen to preaching and teachings from scriptures in your Bible that are printed in red ink only. To hear the Word of Christ is to hear preaching and teachings that have been filtered through the New Covenant of grace and Jesus' finished work. In the Old Testament Christ is concealed; and in the New Testament Christ is revealed. We access God's faith through His Word, and His Word always achieves that which it is meant to accomplish (Isa. 55:11). The degree of faith that you operate in is directly proportional to the revelation knowledge that you have of God through His Word. As a result, many Christians have found it very difficult to operate in faith. This is because they either do not possess a real knowledge of God's Word in them, or they have allowed Satan to steal the Word from them. In the parable recorded in Luke 8:5-8 about the sower and the seed, Jesus portrayed several heart-types, and of these heart-types portrayed, Satan had no direct access to the seed expressed as the Word of God, because Satan cannot steal the Word from us if it is hidden in our hearts (Psa. 119:11). For example, how can you have faith to pray for healing, believing that He will heal you, if you did not know it was God's will for your healing? This is why Satan works so hard to tell the Church today that it may not be God's will for them to be healed! Why? Because it casts doubt, the opposite of faith, in the hearts of God's children! How can you grasp the promises of God, if you do not know what they are? We must first know the truth, then believe it. That is Biblical faith!

Before God's Word can penetrate your heart, you have to understand (not comprehend) what it is saying. If the Word is not understood, then it will be like seed scattered on top of hard-packed ground (the wayside), where the devil can steal it away.

Luke has linked belief and salvation (Luke 8:12) with the Word being sown in our hearts; being similar to what Paul stated in Rom. 10:14-17. If there is no Word, there cannot be any belief or salvation (1 Pet. 1:23). In addition, Luke's use of the word 'saved' could include, but is not necessarily limited to, forgiveness of sins. Salvation includes much more than forgiveness of sins. 'Salvation' in the Hebrew is *yeshuah* (Strong's Expanded Exhaustive Concordance, Hebrew and Aramaic Dictionary Number: 3444), and it means something saved, deliverance, aid, victory, prosperity, health, help, salvation, and welfare. Therefore, Luke could be describing in this verse a believer who simply does not receive the Word in a certain area of his/her life and therefore does not experience the victory that Jesus provided for him/her. We derive the English spelling for Jesus from the root of the Hebrew word *yeshuah*, being *Yeshua*, which means to save, rescue, preserve, and get victory. Once we truly believe in our hearts what God's Word says, we are well on the way to seeing what we believe materialise in the physical realm. For example, once we believe (have faith) that God has made provision for everyone to be healed (Psa. 103:3; Acts 10:38; 1 Pet. 2:24), we can begin to see people healed. If we do not believe that God heals everyone, our hearts become hardened to this truth, we will not see people healed, and we will develop what the Bible calls "...an evil heart of unbelief" (Heb. 3:12). It was unbelief in God's Word that prohibited the Israelites from entering the Promised Land (Heb. 3:18-19), and unbelief will also prevent us benefiting from the "...exceeding great and precious promises..." (2 Pet. 1:2-4) which God has given us in the Scriptures.

2.3 Living and powerful Word of God

The Body of Christ today urgently requires revelation knowledge of the Word of God. To understand what revelation knowledge is and how to get it functional in your life, you have to understand the fundamentals of spirit, soul, and body. Our spirit is that part that changed at salvation. The Bible presents salvation as a life-transforming experience. 2 Cor. 5:17 says "Therefore, if anyone is in Christ, he is a new creation; old things have passed away; behold, all things have become new". Our mind or soul is not born-again with the new birth experience; it has to be renewed (Rom. 12:2). God desires that this salvation be manifest in our physical lives too, and that takes place through the renewing of our minds. This renewing of our minds is a gradual process, affected as we grow in the Lord. The only part of us that is completely changed at salvation (all things are become new, not just some things) is our heart, or spirit, or inward man; which occurs in knowledge after the likeness of Him that created us (Col. 3:10). The Bible shows us that our heart, or spirit, or inward man is complete in Jesus (Eph. 4:24; Col. 2:10). In our spirit, we know all things (1 John 2:20) for we have the mind of Christ (1 Cor. 2:16). But this knowledge will not benefit us physically and mentally until we release this knowledge by renewing our mind. If we think on the same things that the world thinks on, we are going to obtain the same results. If we keep our minds fastened on God through the study of His Word and fellowship with Him, then we will have perfect peace (Isa. 26:3). Rom. 12:2 states "And do not be conformed to this world, but be transformed by the renewing of your mind, that you may prove what is that good and acceptable and perfect will of God". The Greek word that was translated as 'transformed' in this verse is *metamorphoó* (Strong's Expanded Exhaustive Concordance, Greek Dictionary Number: 3339) and is the same word that we get our English word 'metamorphosis' from; and it describes a complete change, like that of a caterpillar changing into a butterfly. This word is also the same word that was used to describe Jesus' transformation when His face shone and His garments became white as the light (Matt 17:2). Bringing our thinking together with God's Word will affect this complete transformation in our lives.

The propulsion for a born-again believer is our spirit, as God enlightens us or leads us through our spirits (Pro. 20:27; Rom. 8:14; 1 Cor. 2:11); but the soul/mind is encouraged by our free will, as we are dominated by our emotions and conscience. Therefore, it is necessary that we get the 'mind of Christ', which is regenerated or made new by the power and working of the Holy Spirit (2 Cor. 5:17), operating in our soul/mind that we can know the will of God, which is good and pleasing to Him, and is perfect (Rom. 12:1). This is done by studying the Word of God, which has been recorded that our soul, mind, will and emotions can understand on a practical level what is being ministered to us spiritually. But according to 2 Cor. 3:6, mere knowledge of God's Word is not enough. We must have spiritual understanding because God's Word is spirit and it is life (John 6:63). As we avail ourselves of God's Word through hearing, meditation and studying, and place it in our heart, the Holy Spirit will regurgitate this knowledge in our spirit at the appropriate time, making the Word of God alive on our inside, and our spirit will bear witness and impart wisdom – revelation knowledge of God's Word – to accomplish a complete and total victory. Having a true revelation of God's Word in our hearts will result in us overcoming this world. The Body of Christ has not realised the authority and capability within God's Word. The knowledge of God's Word has not been abiding in many of us, or the carnal knowledge of the world has choked the Word of God that was there. The Bible warns us that we cannot serve two masters (Matt. 6:24) and that a double-minded man is unstable in all his ways, and cannot receive anything from the Lord (Jas. 1:7-8). If Christians knew these truths, they would spend more time in meditating and studying God's Word, and giving it first place in their heart. Matt. 6:22 gives us the promise that if the eye is single, we will be full of light. That means that if all our attention is focused on God through His Word, then the only thing that we will be full of is God and what His Word produces. This is a spiritual law that is repeated in Rom. 8:6, which says "For to be carnally minded is death, but to be spiritually minded is life and peace". If you are experiencing anything but life and peace, it is because you are carnally minded. You cannot have life and peace without the knowledge of God.

In Heb. 4:12 we are told that "...the word of God is living and powerful...", and to get the Word of God alive and powerful in our lives we need to meditate on His Word. Gal. 5:22 states that faith is a part of the fruit of the Spirit. It is through meditation of the Word of God and the enlightenment of the Holy Spirit that Christ in His fullness is known. The piece of armour known as the "...sword of the Spirit..." (Eph. 6:17) is the only piece of armour that has the ability to cut, wound, and hurt our enemy, the devil. It is not the Bible lying on our bedside table that makes the enemy flee, but rather the Word of God which is hidden in our heart, activated by the Holy Spirit, and spoken in appropriate situations. Have you ever seen a plant struggle to bring forth fruit? Have you ever heard a vine moan and groan and complain about how hard it is to produce grapes? Of course not! It is the nature of a vine to produce grapes. If the vine is protected and given nourishment, it will automatically produce fruit, unless it is starved or attacked by some outside force. So it is with a born-again believer; faith will automatically be the product of our abiding in the Word, which is Jesus (John 1:1; John 15:1-7). Similarly, Jesus said in John 6:63 that "...the words that I speak to you are spirit, and they are life". The Word by itself does not make us free. It is the Word we know, believe and speak that will deliver us (John 8:32). This is because the Word of God has authority, and it supersedes all authority of the Church, of reason, of intellect, and even of Satan himself. Speaking God's Word in faith brings the Holy Spirit into action, and it is He who wields this Word as it is spoken in faith. In Luke 4, when Jesus was tempted of the devil for forty days, it was the Word of God that Jesus used to defeat the enemy in the time of His temptation.

Jesus constantly met His temptation by quoting from God's Word as He repeatedly stated the phrase "It is written...".

There are times when our enthusiasm to learn God's Word prohibits us from allowing the mind of Christ in our spirit to absorb the power contained in His Word, and realise and develop the authority and capability within the Word. We would be better off with only a fraction of God's Word in us, which we have a revelation knowledge of, than if we had a broad awareness of Scripture, but with only a carnal understanding. The early disciples are an example of this, because in comparison to the completed Word of God that we have today, they did not have the majority of the New Testament scriptures, and the Old Covenant scriptures were not readily available to them, and yet they still transformed their present-day world. I am not proposing that we stop reading the Word of God and satisfy ourselves with the knowledge of the Word, but we need to recognise that when God's Word is combined with faith (Rom. 10:10), only then will it profit us (Heb. 4:2) through the enlightenment of the Holy Spirit. Paul said in 1 Cor. 4:20, "For the kingdom of God is not in word but in power". You are not incapable of living a life of faith. Quite the contrary, as a born-again believer, you have already been given THE measure of faith as a part of the fruit of the Holy Spirit. Gal. 5:22-23 says "But the fruit of the Spirit is love, joy, peace, longsuffering, gentleness, goodness, **faith**, meekness, temperance: against such there is no law" (KJV, emphasis mine). We have all been given the measure of faith (Rom. 12:3), but continue to be defeated because of a lack of knowledge of how that faith works. Peter, writing to fellow Christians, opens his second epistle with "...To those who have obtained **like precious faith** with us by the righteousness of our God and Savior Jesus Christ" (2 Pet. 1:1) (emphasis mine). No Christian receives more or less faith than any other Christian because it takes the same amount of faith to get saved, and that amount is called the measure of faith.

Mankind did not learn how to fly overnight. There were many failures, but now no one doubts that the laws of aerodynamics work. Likewise, you will not learn all God's laws pertaining to faith overnight either; you may fail a few times before you start seeing faith produce that which it should. The law of faith, which created everything, is without a doubt more certain than the laws of aerodynamics. The knowledge of God and how faith works is hidden for you, not from you, in the Word of God. If you are of the opinion that you require the knowledge of God, then pray this prayer as recorded in Eph. 1:15-21:

Heavenly Father, I ask that You give me the spirit of wisdom and revelation in the knowledge of You, that my understanding will be renewed; that I may know what it is that You require me to do for Your Kingdom, realise what You have provided me by grace through Jesus, and may abound and increase yet more and more through the knowledge of Your exceeding love toward me. I ask this according to the incredible greatness of Your power, being the same mighty power that raised Jesus Christ from the dead and seated Him in a place of honour at Your right hand in the heavenly realms, being far above all principality and power and might and dominion, and every name that is named, not only in this age but also in that which is to come. In Jesus name, Amen.

Now, believe that you receive, and watch faith begin to be produced in your life.

2.4 The measure of faith

We have the same faith that Paul had. Paul said in Gal. 2:20, "I am crucified with Christ: nevertheless I live; yet not I, but Christ liveth in me: and the life which I now live in the flesh I live by the **faith of the Son of God**, who loved me, and gave himself for me" (emphasis mine). Firstly, I am quoting from the King James

Version of the Bible as almost every modern English translation misinterpreted this verse from Greek and made it read, 'faith in Christ'. The commentaries have led us to believe that the phrase 'faith of the Son of God' is really just an odd way of saying 'faith in Christ' and that it really refers to our faith in Christ. But such reckless handling of the Word of God, be it deliberate or otherwise, completely alters the meaning of the God-inspired scriptures. Paul did not say that he lived by faith **IN** the Son of God, but by the faith **OF** the Son of God. The measure of faith that Paul had was the same measure that Jesus had. We could never be saved by our faith in Christ, were it not for the faith of Christ; and we can never be saved by the faith of Christ until we have faith in Christ. Yes, we must have faith in Christ; and our faith in Christ is the result of 'the faith of Christ' as our Saviour in this world. In addition, 'the faith of the Son of God' is referring to Jesus' faithful performance of all the Father wills as our covenant Surety, Substitute and Redeemer. Therefore, if there is only one measure of faith (Rom. 12:3), then we also have the faith of Jesus. Faith does not come and go as many Christians think; it is constant. What does fluctuate, however, is (a) our perception of whether or not we have faith, and (b) how much faith we use or manifest. Notice, however, that in Rom. 12:3 Paul was writing to Believers. He wrote "...to everyone who is among you...". The epistle of Romans was a letter to Christians. He addresses this letter "To all who are in Rome, beloved of God, called to be saints..." (Rom. 1:7) and not to everyone that is in the world.

We have the same quantity and quality of faith that Jesus has; therefore, we can do the same works that Jesus did, if we receive this truth and begin to use what we have (John 14:12). Because many Christians have not understood this, they have spent their time asking for faith or for more faith. How is God going to answer a prayer like that? For example, if I gave you the keys to my car and then you turned around and asked me if you could use my car, what should I say to you? I would probably stand there surprised while I tried to figure out what you actually wanted, as I have given you the keys to my car and therefore, indirectly, given you permission to use my car. That is the reason there is not an answer from God when we plead with Him for faith, or more faith. We already have the same faith Jesus has. There is nothing more that God can give us! Paul, writing to the Church in Corinth, includes himself and therefore we can believe that the statement applies to all Christians, states: "And since we have the same spirit of faith, according to what is written, 'I believed and therefore I spoke', we also believe and therefore speak" (2 Cor. 4:13). Paul says that "...we **have** the same spirit of faith..." (emphasis mine), and not that we must strive for, request, pray about, or hope for... we have it! Also, we have the spirit of faith "...according to what is written...", being the same kind of faith that Jesus spoke about in Mark 11:22-24. You may encounter someone quoting from Paul's second letter to the Thessalonians where he wrote "...for not all have faith" (2 Thes. 3:2). Yet in Rom. 12:3 Paul writes "...God hath dealt to every man the measure of faith". Looking at these two verses (being only a part of a verse and taken out of context) it seems that Paul is contradicting himself, and that person may state that Paul was confused and this is the evidence. But when you read the entire verse of 2 Thes. 3:2 you will realise that Paul is referring to the ungodly, and not Believers. Not everyone that is in the world has the God-kind of faith; whereas all Believers have the God-kind of faith. The same faith that God used to create the worlds in the beginning is a permanent part of our born-again spirit. Yet there are Christians praying for more faith. Mark 11:23 says "For assuredly, I say to you, whoever says to this mountain, 'Be removed and be cast into the sea', and does not doubt in his heart, but believes that those things he says will be done, he will have whatever he says'". This faith that Jesus is talking about is the God-kind of faith, or God's supernatural faith, or the Abraham-kind of faith; and every believer already has the measure of this kind of faith. You do not have to search for it; you do not have to pray for it; you do not have to fast for it; and you do not have to promise to do greater and better works to get it. You already have it! Eph. 2:8 states "For by grace you have been saved through faith, and that not of yourselves; it is the gift of God". If we did not receive from God **THE** measure of faith, it would be impossible for us to be saved, as this faith by which we were saved was not of ourselves, it was not natural human faith. The instant we are saved, a change occurs within our heart, or spirit, or our inward man. We receive a new spirit and our new spirit becomes one with God's Spirit (1 Cor. 6:17). The Holy Spirit constantly produces faith (Gal. 5:22); therefore, within our new spirit is all the faith we will ever need (Col. 2:10).

Although we all have been given **THE** measure of faith, Jesus did say that He had never seen such great faith as the centurion manifested (Matt. 8:10), and He also spoke of His disciples' little faith (Matt. 8:26). But He was speaking about how much faith He saw being used. None of us use all the faith we have been given. In that sense, some do have more faith than others, but technically, it is more faith that is being exhibited or that is functional. Most Christians do not doubt that faith works. They just doubt that they have enough faith. The more you know about faith and how it works, the better it will work for you. If all you knew was that you have the same faith Jesus has, then that would remove hopelessness and motivate you. If Satan can blind you to this truth, then he can keep you from using the faith you have. I once heard someone say that you either have faith or you don't. But that is incorrect, as you can have more or less faith as I mentioned above. You decide what to do with the measure of faith God has given you. 2 Thes. 1:3 says "We are bound to thank God always for you, brethren, as it is fitting, because your faith grows exceedingly...". Therefore, if faith is measurable, it can be either great or small, more or less. Jesus made several comments about faith: to Peter walking on the water He said "...O you of little faith, why did you doubt?"; to the centurion who came to Him on behalf of his servant He said "...I have not found such great faith, not even in Israel". In Rom. 4:19-20 we read about faith being both strong and weak. Jas. 2:5 says "...Has God not chosen the poor of this world to be rich in faith...", and in Jas. 2:22 we read of a perfect faith. In Acts 6:5, Luke records that Stephen was full of faith. The first epistle of Paul to Timothy refers to sincere faith (1 Tim. 1:5) and shipwrecked faith (1 Tim. 1:19). Finally, we read in 1 John 5:4 about overcoming faith.

God did not give us different measures of faith; we all received **THE** measure of faith. If I were serving soup to a group of people, and if I used the same serving spoon to dish it out, then that serving spoon would be **THE** measure. Everyone would get the same amount of soup because I would use the same measure. That is the way it is with God's supernatural faith. He only used one measure. Paul reminds us in Rom. 2:11 that "...there is no partiality with God". All born-again Christians received the same amount of faith. There is just a lack of knowing and using what God has already given us. Through the reading of the Word of God, and having that revelation knowledge hidden in your heart activated by the Holy Spirit, you will have the ability to change your circumstances and move those mountains in your life. We as believers must avail ourselves of God's Word by placing it in our heart, so that the Holy Spirit may bring it forth at the appropriate time to accomplish a complete and total victory.

Chapter 3

Putting Faith into Practice

3.1 Introduction

As we have seen in the previous chapter, every Christian already has **THE** measure of the God-kind of faith. Rom. 2:11 reassures us that "...there is no partiality with God"; as a born-again believer, you have already been given THE measure of faith as part of the fruit of the Holy Spirit. Gal. 5:22-23 says "But the fruit of the Spirit is love, joy, peace, longsuffering, gentleness, goodness, **faith**, meekness, temperance: against such there is no law" (KJV, emphasis mine). Unfortunately, many Christians have done with their measure of faith the same as the servant did with the talent he received from his master (Matt. 25:25). It is up to us what we do with the measure of faith God has given us, and it will grow or increase according to what we do with our measure of faith. We are in direct control of its growth, not God.

3.2 Eating correctly

It is without doubt that God has provided the means whereby your faith can be increased; but the measure of faith that was given to you can only increase when you (a) feed your faith with the Word of God, and (b) exercise your faith or put it into practice! This can be likened to consuming good food regularly, which improves your health and long-term well-being. But without exercise this good food can lead to weight gain, which has serious health consequences. We need to feed our faith with God's Word, and exercise our faith in order to change our circumstances and move those mountains in our lives. Fred Francis Bosworth, an evangelist, once said 'most Christians feed their bodies three square meals each day but only feed their spirits one cold snack each week.... Then they wonder why they are so weak in faith'. Imagine if we fed our body only one cold snack a day. Without the necessary food and nutrients to function and help get through the day, our bodies will begin to fatigue and eventually it will go into survival mode, resulting in declining health and possible fatality. Yet there are many Christians today wondering why they are suffering spiritual infirmities.

The more you know about faith and how it works, the better it will work for you. By continuing to grow your faith, you will eventually see results; but we often give up too easily because we believe we do not have what it takes. God has given us everything we need, including all the faith we need. We need to acknowledge what we have and begin to learn God's laws pertaining to faith. There is no lack of faith within any Christian. There is just a lack of knowing and using what God has already given us. Phm. 1:6 says "...that the sharing of your faith may become effective by the acknowledgment of every good thing which is in you in Christ Jesus". Notice that Paul was not praying that Philemon would obtain something more from the Lord, but rather that his faith would begin to work as he acknowledged what he already had. The word 'acknowledge' in the Greek is *epignósis* (Strong's Expanded Exhaustive Concordance, Greek Dictionary Number: 1922), and it means perception, discernment, recognition, intuition. You can only acknowledge something that you already have. We already have the faith of God, and it will begin to work when we acknowledge this. When you take the time to feed on the Word of God, faith will arise in your spirit because Jesus said "...The words that I speak to you are spirit, and they are life" (John 6:63). You will receive revelation knowledge when reading and meditating on the Word. A lack of knowledge will hinder you and keep you in bondage because you cannot act on God's Word beyond actual knowledge of God's Word. Faith will grow with an understanding of the Word. If your faith is not growing, then it can be assumed that your understanding of the Word is not growing. A lack of knowledge of what God's Word says, a lack of knowledge of our redemption, and a lack of knowledge of our redemptive rights in Christ Jesus are often the reasons for unbelief.

3.3 A man of few words

There is something about Jesus you may not have noticed, even if you have read the New Testament many times. It relates to a characteristic, or practice, that consistently marked His ministry on earth. I have never heard anyone else mention this observation, but Jesus was a man of few words; and in my opinion this is a characteristic, or practice that we as Christians should adopt and apply, especially in crucial and complex situations. A study of the Gospels reveals that whenever He spoke a faith command, whether He was dealing with circumstances, sickness, death or the devil, He kept it brief. Jesus healed a leper by declaring "...I am willing; be cleansed..." (Matt. 8:3; Mark 1:41; Luke 5:13). He calmed a raging storm at sea by speaking "...Peace, be still!..." (Mark 4:39). He raised Lazarus by simply saying "...Lazarus, come forth!". In Matt. 21:19 we read of where Jesus transformed a fig tree in full bloom to a shrivelled remnant with: "...Let no fruit grow on you ever again". When it came to teaching, Jesus could talk for the entire day. But when He activated His faith, spoken with boldness, He kept it simple... and He always saw results! Can you imagine how the average believer today would deal with a fig tree like the one in Mark 11? I can almost guarantee that even a Christian who knows something about living by faith would not stop after one sentence. It would probably be something to the effect of: 'Tree, in the Name of Jesus, the name above all names and the Creator of heaven and earth, by the power and authority vested in me, being the righteousness of God in Christ, you are cursed. Your leaves are going to whither and fall off. Your bark is going to peel. You are going to shrivel up. Tree, I declare that you are finished and dead!' And if that does not work, there are alternative options involving a blade or poison, and unbelief.... I am sure that you have heard and seen this before, maybe even done it yourself. I know that I have. But, praise God, we have Jesus' example to follow. We can learn to operate in faith like He did, with few words filled with faith.

There may be some people that will say that we cannot imitate Jesus as we do not possess His abilities. But through the new birth, we have been born of the Word and spiritually re-created in Jesus' image. The Bible clearly says "...as He is, so are we in this world" (1 John 4:17); therefore we must have the same spiritual capability that He has. The dilemma is there are many Christians that neither understand the fundamentals of faith, nor know how faith works. These Christians have heard just enough of the so-called 'faith message' to make them dangerous, exuding words 'of faith' like spray paint from a can and hoping some of these 'faith' statements will coat their problems and or desires. Look at Mark 11 again, but this time go beyond Jesus talking to the fig tree and teaching His disciples about faith, Jesus going into the temple, overturning the money-changers' tables and driving out the merchants, and Jesus talking and acting as a man of faith and power, and notice verse 11. It describes the day before Jesus said anything to the fig tree or overturned the money-changers' tables: "And Jesus went into Jerusalem and into the temple. So when He had looked around at all things, as the hour was already late, He went out to Bethany with the twelve". Jesus spent time in the temple just listening and not talking, observing and not acting. I am of the opinion that He was seeking His Father's will and how God wanted Him to handle the situation. I say this because Jesus said that He only did what He saw the Father do, and He only said what He heard the Father say (John 5:19, John 14:10).

Reading the account leading up to Jesus' last Passover week (Mark 11:1-11), you will notice that He went by the fig tree that day without saying a word to it. He entered the temple and watched the money-changers without making His presence known. I am convinced that He was incensed by what was going on there that day as He was the next day, but that day He neither did anything nor said anything. That night, He went back to Bethany and prayed until He heard from God what He was supposed to say, and saw in His spirit what He was supposed to do. The next morning on His way back to Jerusalem, and seeing the fig tree in full blossom, an indication that the figs should be ripe to eat (figs normally appear on the tree before the leaves), Jesus approached the fig tree. "And seeing from afar a fig tree having leaves, He went to see if perhaps He would find something on it. When He came to it, He found nothing but leaves, for it was not the season for figs. In response Jesus said to it, 'Let no one eat fruit from you ever again'" (Mark 11:13-14). Jesus spoke the desired end results to that tree and nothing else. As far as He was concerned, from that moment on, His act of faith was past tense and so was the fig tree. After He had cursed the fig tree, He turned His back on it, travelled on to Jerusalem, drove out the money-changers and merchants from the temple, and then spent the remainder of the day in Jerusalem preaching (Mark 11:19). Jesus was not just reacting to the moment. He was operating in union with the Father, according to the instructions He had received the day before. On their way back to Bethany, Jesus and His disciples passed by the fig tree, several hours after He had cursed it, but there was no visible change to the fig tree. But it is important to perceive and understand what was taking place. A course of action was proceeding as a result of Jesus' faith-filled words spoken, but the effectiveness of His faith had not become evident to the disciples' physical senses.

The following morning Peter noticed what the disciples had probably been watching for ever since Jesus had spoken to that fig tree; "...as they passed by, they saw the fig tree dried up from the roots. And Peter, remembering, said to Him, 'Rabbi, look! The fig tree which You cursed has withered away'. So Jesus answered and said to them, 'Have faith in God'" (Mark 11:20-22). With His answer, Jesus not only commanded His disciples to do what He did, but He presented them with the faith by which the Just should live (Rom. 1:17; Gal. 3:11). The word 'just' in the Greek is *dikaiŏs* (Strong's Expanded Exhaustive Concordance, Greek Dictionary Number: 1342), and it means righteous, a state of being righteous, doing right, in right standing with God. Therefore, we as born-again believers, being declared righteous in Christ, 'shall live' by faith (Hab. 2:4; Heb. 10:38). In other words, faith should be a way of life, or a lifestyle. After this, Jesus continued and taught them how faith works: "For assuredly, I say to you, whoever says to this mountain, 'Be removed and be cast into the sea', and does not doubt in his heart, but believes that those things he says will be done, he will have whatever he says" (Mark 11:23). In all things, Jesus is our example. We are to place the same value on words as He did; words anointed and inspired by God. If Jesus places a high standard on the words that He speaks, then we need to be thoughtful about the words we speak. Through actions Jesus showed us to speak the desired outcome, and then turn around and walk off, expecting those words spoken to come to pass. If we speak words of faith and then say 'it does not look to me like anything is happening', we disconnect from faith and abort the process. Knowing what to say in any situation will become obvious as you draw near to the One referred to in Heb. 3:1 as the Apostle and High Priest of our profession, Christ Jesus. Ask Him about the situation, saying 'Lord, it seems to me that the desired outcome here is such and such. Is that correct?'. Then, listen on the inside of you (being your inward man, heart, or spirit) to hear what He says. When you start doing this, you will discover how easy it is to discern the voice of God. When Jesus, your High Priest, tells you what to say, as far as heaven, all the angels, and all the demons of hell are concerned, it is as if Jesus Himself is speaking; and when He speaks, we should expect to see the miraculous power of God manifest in our lives. Follow the example of our Master, who so often was, and is, a Man of few words.

3.4 Boldly proclaim your faith

Looking at the account of Jesus and the fig tree again in Mark 11, I am certain that there may be some Christians that, when they curse a tree they may do so silently in the event that the curse does not work, at least no one would have heard them and therefore no one would know about their act of faith, thereby avoiding any possible embarrassment. But Jesus spoke aloud, loud enough for His disciples to hear. That is confidence and boldness of faith. He had absolute faith in what He said; knowing that what He said would come to pass; and it did.

Faith is an action; it is action requiring you to accept God's Word as true. Isa. 55:11 states "So shall My word be that goes forth from My mouth; It shall not return to Me void, but it shall accomplish what I please, and it shall prosper in the thing for which I sent it". There is always an opportunity for you to positively act on God's Word, even if it is simply thanking and praising Him that He has heard your prayer. When you begin believing God's Word as the absolute truth, you will begin seeing the desired results. It does not matter how much faith you have, if you do not exercise your measure of faith, there will be no results. Consider the crippled man at Lystra. In Acts 14:7-9 we read "And in Lystra a certain man without strength in his feet was sitting, a cripple from his mother's womb, who had never walked. This man heard Paul speaking. Paul, observing him intently and seeing that **he had faith to be healed**" (emphasis mine). Every believer has faith to be healed, but you have to act on your faith for it to work for you. The Bible tells us how to put our faith in action in Mark 11:23. You act on your faith, or exercise it by saying what you believe. Faith cannot be released out of your heart toward God without your saying what you believe. Faith simply will not work without an expression or action. Nowhere in the Bible do you ever read that faith was released apart from an action. Faith that is only in your heart will never bring healing to your body, or the infilling of the Holy Spirit, or even an answer to prayer. Only faith in your heart released through your speaking will! Jesus said "...whoever... does not **doubt in his heart**, but believes that those things he says will be done, he will have whatever he says" (Mark 11:23). Paul perceived that the disabled man in Acts 14 had faith. Paul did not perceive his own faith, but that of the disabled man. This man had faith to be healed. He got faith from what he heard Paul preach (Rom. 10:17). Paul understood that faith without action or works is dead (Jas. 2:18, 20, 22). Paul also knew he was going to have to get the man to act on the faith that he had. In Acts 14:10 Paul said "...Stand up straight on your feet!". When Paul gave the command in faith, the impotent man combined the action of standing with his faith, and the Bible says "...he leaped and walked".

In Mark 11:23 we are told three times to 'say', and only once to 'believe'. From this it is evident that you have to confidently believe, which will cause you to speak out what you believe in your heart, and you will have whatever you say. This is a spiritual law. It will work for anybody. If you say it and believe it when you say it, it will be yours; you will have what you say. Getting healing, receiving the Holy Spirit, or even getting an answer to prayer, requires a believing part and an action part. If you act without faith, nothing will happen. If you believe without acting, again, nothing will happen. However, when faith and action are brought together, then the Word of God works. There is nothing complicated about faith; it is as effortless as the Word of God says it is! Reading on in Mark 11:24, Jesus is talking, and says "...whatever things you ask when you pray, believe that you receive them, and you will have them". In the King James Version of the Bible this scripture says "...what things soever ye desire...". You may wonder what does the 'things' mean or comprise of. I believe that Jesus was referring to physical possessions such as cars (or donkeys in Jesus' time), houses, furniture, clothes, appliances, and so forth as these are classified as things. Then regarding desire... I have heard it said that God will not give you the desires of your heart; He will only meet your needs, not your desires; and hence we should pray, 'if it be Your will' and avoid getting into the flesh as it is not what we desire, but rather what God desires for us. But the Bible recorded Jesus saying "...desire...". Also, Psa. 37:4 states "Delight yourself also in the Lord, and He shall give you the **desires** of your heart" (emphasis mine). In the Old Testament God promises under the Old Covenant to give His people the desires of their heart, and the New Covenant is a better covenant, based on better promises (Heb. 8:6), and if the Old Testament saints could obtain their desires under the Old Covenant, then how much more can we get the desires of our heart under the New Covenant? That said, I am certain that there are Christians who may deliberate the result of desiring the wrong thing, and whether they would indeed receive whatever they desire even if it was wrong. My only comment would be that if you are filled with the Holy Spirit, and are being led by the Spirit, why would you ask for something that would be either hurtful, harmful, or separate you from the love of God? We need to have as much faith in ourselves as God has in us. Jesus had so much faith in us when He said "...desire..." (Mark 11:24) that, in effect, He gave us this so-called signed blank cheque for us to use. There may also be some Christians not prepared to use this so-called signed blank cheque as they are concerned that they may desire and receive something they do not know whether it is good or not for them. Again, my only comment would be that if you do not know whether it is good for you or not, then you have no business asking for it. This would be similar to someone wanting to buy their child a kitten for his/her birthday, and approaching a person standing by the side of the road selling what seems to be a litter of kittens. Not knowing the difference between a lion cub and an alley cat, you are better off buying him/her a dog; this will save you much trouble when the 'cat' starts to grow. In 2 Pet. 1:3 Peter said "...His divine power has given to us **all things** that pertain to life and godliness, through the knowledge of Him who called us by glory and virtue..." (emphasis mine). The law of faith always works. If you believe that God will, then He will; and if you believe that God will not, then He will not (Mark 9:23). You have the right to believe for anything God's Word promises, and therefore, whatever you believe for will transpire when supported by Scripture. The Bible says that we are to believe that we receive it, and we shall have it (Mark 11:24). It all comes down to what we believe. However, believing for things outside or beyond the promises of God is presumption, or foolishness. Faith is based on God's Word, and without it there is no foundation for your faith.

The New Testament word 'desire' in the Greek is *aiteó* (Strong's Expanded Exhaustive Concordance, Greek Dictionary Number: 154), and it means to ask or to request. Therefore, according to this promise what will God give you... your desires, what you pray for, what you ask for? Certainly not! You will only receive what you believe you received when you prayed. If you believe you receive a better job when you pray for a better job, you will receive a better job. But if you ask for a better job but you do not believe you received a better job when you prayed, you will not get a better job. When I pray and ask God for a better job, but with doubt in my heart that I will not get a better job, and I then subsequently do not get a better job, can I say that God answered my prayer? Yes! I asked for a better job, but I believed I would receive nothing, and I got nothing; so in fact I got exactly what I believed for, namely nothing. Therefore, my prayer was answered. Remember, faith is the evidence of things not seen or perceived by your physical senses. If I had to ask you whether you believe you have a right leg, what would you say? Can you see your right leg? I am sure you can see (or you would not be reading this book). Then, if faith is the evidence of things not seen, why then would you believe you have a right leg if you can see your right leg.... The word 'receive' in Mark 11:24 is a Greek aorist tense which is very often translated as a simple past tense in English. Almost every modern English translation of this verse places 'receive' in the past tense, which in my opinion is the correct translation, meaning that you are to believe that you have already received that which you are asking for. If you believe you have already received what you asked for, then tomorrow when you pray, do not ask again! If you believe you have already received, then how can you ask again? If you ask again, then that is an indication that you did not believe you received that which you asked for when you prayed the first time. Rather, thank God every time you pray for that which you asked for until it manifests, becomes clear or obvious to the eye or your mind, appears plainly to the eye, and becomes evident. Some may highlight Jesus' parable recorded in Luke 18:1-8 about the unjust judge and state that this parable proves that we are to, like the woman, persistently nag God until we receive that which we asked for. But this is not what Jesus was conveying. This parable is similar to the one recorded in Luke 11:5-13 and what Jesus is trying to communicate to us is that if this woman could get what she wanted from an unjust judge, for no other reason than the fact that she persisted, how much more can we expect to receive from our heavenly Father with whom we have a blood-bought right to act on our faith. In addition, perceive the rest of the verse; it says, "...believe that you receive them, and you will have them". The 'will have' is future tense, signifying that when you believe you have received what you asked for when you first prayed, there is no physical evidence of that which you asked for, otherwise you would not have needed to ask for it. In other words, although you believe you have received it, you will only physically be in a position, sometime in the future, where you can demonstrate/illustrate that which you asked for to others. But, in the meantime, while you wait for the physical manifestation of that which you asked for, you have to believe that you have already received it.

Do not let this confuse you. Think of faith in the following manner: you attend an interview for a job, and your new employer says to you 'congratulations, we think that you are the ideal candidate and we would like to offer you the job. In exchange for working for us, we will pay you GBP 5,000 per month'. Would you then say to your new employer 'I do not believe anything I cannot see; I would like to audit your accounts to confirm that you can afford to pay me GBP 5,000 per month'? Of course not. You act like a trained dog, and come to work every day for a whole month, and during that time you never see any money. You accepted what your new employer said to you... how is it that you can believe the word of a carnal minded person yet you cannot believe the word of Your heavenly Father? If anyone was to defraud the company and make off to a remote island with the payroll before the month-end, it would be a man, not your heavenly Father. Some sceptics may ask how you can believe that you have received what you cannot see. Well, have you seen your brain? Yet you believe that you have a brain...; or you go to DFS Furniture Holdings plc, select and pay for a new sofa, which they tell you will be delivered within five weeks. Then over the next five weeks, every time you have family and friends visiting, you tell them all about the new sofa you have purchased, which obviously you cannot show to them until after the five weeks have ended. The only evidence that you have to prove that the sofa you paid for belongs to you is the contract or receipt you received from DFS Furniture Holdings plc, being a piece of paper. That is exactly the same for faith. While you are waiting for that which you asked God for to manifest itself, the proof or evidence that you have received is the promise in the Word of God. Your faith is anchored on that promise in the Word of God and that is the evidence that you have what you asked God for until that which you asked for manifests itself, then you do not need the evidence anymore as you are now in physical possession of that which you asked for when you prayed.

3.5 Patience

We all want good things to happen in our lives, but too often we want it now... not later. God wants us to live by discernment, acquired through revelation knowledge, and not head knowledge. As a result, it can be difficult to exercise discernment without trusting God. Trusting God often requires not knowing how God is going to accomplish what needs to be done and not knowing when He will do it. We often say God is never late, but generally He is not early either. Why? Because He uses times of waiting to stretch our faith in Him and to bring about the necessary change and growth required in our lives. Patience is a spiritual force that supports your faith, similar to the way a table leg supports the table, or the roots support a tree. But Satan also tries that which you call 'faith' to see if it is true faith, based on revelation knowledge, or if it is merely head knowledge. Peter said "...do not think it strange concerning the fiery trial which is to try you, as though some strange thing happened to you; but rejoice to the extent that you partake of Christ's sufferings..." (1 Peter 4:12-13). It is definitely not strange that these things happen. Like me, I am in no doubt that you have heard people say that 'God tries and tests your faith to perfect it', and often support this statement by misquoting Rom. 8:28 by saying 'God makes all things work together for the good'. Trials are a design of Satan, not God; and Satan is not out to perfect your faith. For if the trying of your faith perfected it, all Christians would be in a better place as I do not know of anyone who has not experienced, and probably is still experiencing, trials or tests....

In Luke 22:31-32 Jesus said to Peter "...Satan has asked for you, that he may sift you as wheat. But I have prayed for you, that your faith should not fail...". Notice these verses do not say 'God has asked for you, that He may sift you' but rather that 'Satan has asked for you'. This word 'asked' in the Greek is *exaiteó* (Strong's Expanded Exhaustive Concordance, Greek Dictionary Number: 1809), and means demanded. Satan had demanded to have Peter that he might sift him or test him. So often Christians think God is doing the sifting and the trying of their faith, that they humbly bow down and bear the trials and tests. They suffer whatever comes their way because they believe it is God perfecting them. But Jas. 1:3 says "...the testing of your faith produces **patience**" (emphasis mine). And Paul did write in Rom. 8:28 that "...all things work together for good to those who love God...", but we need to understand the context of what Paul was teaching. The scripture reads "Likewise the Spirit also helps in our weaknesses. For we do not know what we should pray for as we ought, but the Spirit Himself makes intercession for us with groanings which cannot be uttered. Now He who searches the hearts knows what the mind of the Spirit is, because He makes intercession for the saints according to the will of God. And we know that all things work together for good to those who love God, to those who are the called according to His purpose. (Rom. 8:26-28). Paul was saying that after you have prayed in the spirit, then you know that all things you prayed about through inter-cession in the spirit will work together for good.

If you really believe that God is the one sending trials or tests to perfect your faith, you should embrace and be supportive of those trials or tests, as all attempts to alleviate those trials or tests will be in direct disagreement with God's will and perfect plan for your life. This is similar to believing that God is the one who places poverty, sickness, and adversity on Christians because He is trying to work some good in their lives. In my opinion, this is not the abundant life promised to us in God's Word, nor what Jesus was crucified for. The belief that God controls everything independent of our free will is probably the biggest inroad we give Satan into our lives as we become passive in resisting him and do not exercise our faith. Satan is not the finisher of your faith, and if trials and tests perfected faith, Satan would be the finisher of it. Heb. 12:2 declares that Jesus is the author and finisher of your faith. In Matt. 6 we read about Jesus teaching His disciples a model for prayer. Reading Matt. 6:9-10 it says "...Our Father in heaven, Hallowed be Your name. Your kingdom come. Your will be done on earth as it is in heaven...". Stop there and ask yourself whether it is God's will that we be tested and tried in heaven? Jesus asserted that it is the Father's will for things to be done on earth, as they are done in heaven. In heaven there are neither tests, trials, sickness, poverty, nor lack. Therefore, it is not God's will for you to be tested and tried, have sickness, poverty, and or lack in this life! In Matt. 26:41 Jesus said to His disciples "Watch and pray, lest you enter into temptation...". The word 'temptation' in the Greek is *peirasmos* (Strong's Expanded Exhaustive Concordance, Greek Dictionary Number: 3986), and it means trial, probation, or testing. This word is the same word translated trial and test in other parts of the New Testament. For that reason, we can rephrase Jas. 1:13 to read as follows: "Let no one say when he is tried and tested, 'I am tried and tested by God'; for God cannot be tried and tested by evil, nor does He Himself try and test anyone".

The Bible tells us in Rom. 15:4 where patience comes from: "For whatever things were written before were written for our learning, that we through the patience and comfort of the Scriptures might have hope". As we develop patience, the Bible confirms that we will feel completely satisfied, lacking nothing (Jas. 1:4). A patient person is powerful; they remain calm in a storm, have control over their mouths, and their thoughts remain loving in times when the behaviour of others becomes challenging. Like patience, our relationship with God involves progressive change. We learn to trust God by going through many experiences that require trust. The proof that we trust God is to refuse to worry. However, learning to trust the One who knows all things entails accepting that some questions may never be answered. By seeing God's faithfulness manifest itself over and over, we evolve from a state of trusting ourselves to gradually placing our trust in Him. God does not always reveal to us the exact timing of His will and perfect plan for our lives. Although frustrating, not knowing the exact timing is often what helps us to persevere and hang on. If we knew how long it was going to take, we might give up. But when we accept God's timing, we can learn to live in hope and enjoy our lives while God is working on our problems and desires. We know that God's plan for our lives is good, and when we entrust ourselves to Him, we can experience total peace and happiness. Without patience we cannot continue to see the fulfilment of our faith. Everything does not come to us immediately by believing. There is a waiting period when one is involved in receiving from God. It is during that period that our faith is tested and purified. Only if we continue and wait patiently will we experience the joy of seeing what we have believed for. Without great patience, there is no great faith. Without great faith, there are no great victories. You will not achieve any victory without a battle. That is why the Christian lifestyle is called the fight of faith. There are many people who can impress with their ability to recite scriptures, but they are not too keen to get involved in the fight and step on Satan's toes. When they exercise their faith and nothing happens immediately, they begin destroying everything that was established by their measure of faith through doubting, not believing, being impatient, and they promptly relinquish the good fight. Patience in the hard times is what develops true faith. That is why James said to "...count it all joy when you fall into various trials, knowing that the testing of your faith produces patience. But let patience have its perfect work, that you may be perfect and complete, lacking nothing" (Jas. 1:2-4). You can count it joy because you know that as you endure and stand firm in faith, your faith is developing and becoming stronger. You are not rejoicing over the problem, or thanking God for the trial; you are thanking Him and rejoicing in the fact that He is going to deliver you.

No one has ever received anything from God in the natural or in the spiritual realm without showing some patience. You cannot succeed at anything in the secular world without patience. Faith is no get-rich-quick scheme. The reason some Christians never receive anything from God, including answers to their prayers, is because they quit too soon. Their faith runs out. The Bible says that it is through faith and patience that we inherit the promises (Heb. 6:12). Everyone likes the faith part, but they want to ignore and thereby avoid the patience part. If they could, they would remove the word 'patience' out of their Bible. When someone is sick, a thermometer is used to measure their temperature. In the same way, the level of our patience is a measure of our spiritual maturity. Patience is simply faith applied over a prolonged period of time. Instead of a momentary faith, patience is prolonged, enduring faith. Patience is when you just believe and keep believing. Just as patience comes through the Word of God, so does faith. They are both fruits of the Spirit (Gal. 5:22). When you were born again, God gave you faith and patience. They are fruits of your brand-new, born-again spirit. Similar to farming, there is always a waiting period between sowing and harvesting. After a seed is planted, heat from the sun, moisture, and the pressure of the fertile soil causes the dry outer covering of that seed to burst open, and roots shoot out into the fertile soil. But this process takes time to happen, and it happens underground. Above the ground, there is no evidence that anything is happening. This process can be likened to our faith. After we plant seeds of obedience and trust, we cannot sense that anything is happening; but on the inside (the inward man, or the heart, or the spirit) much is taking place. Resembling the green shoot that bursts from the seed and through the ground, so our seed of obedience and trust reveals our faith as a believing response to God, producing the desires of our heart. Patience is not only the ability to wait, but also the ability to keep a good attitude while waiting. Waiting is part of life and cannot be avoided. We spend much of our lives waiting, and if we do not learn to do it well, we will be despondent. God is patient with us, and we are to imitate Him (3 John 1:11). Be encouraged to actively pursue patience, it will lead you into God's power.

3.6 Using faith to access God's grace

When Jesus came, He brought in a new dispensation, and although the Old Testament Law did not pass away (Matt. 5:17-18), those who placed their faith in Jesus were no longer subject to the Law (Rom. 6:14; Gal. 3:24-25). Jesus is God's grace (being God's undeserved, unearned and unmerited favour), and Paul confirms that we gain access to God's grace through faith in Jesus (Rom. 5:2; 1 Cor. 1:4; Eph. 2:7-8). Grace is not a Bible subject, nor a doctrine, but rather the person, the Lord Jesus Christ (Rom. 5:17). There is only one gospel, and that is the Gospel of the Lord Jesus Christ, or the Gospel of grace, which will bring you blessings, such as healing, prosperity, success, salvation, right-eousness, protection, security, peace and wholeness, and this is only the beginning... it will bring you much, much more! If the blessings of God were subject to us keeping the Law, then we would warrant, deserve, and justify His favour. It would be our reward. But grace is underserved, unearned and unmerited. Some ministers teach that to fall from grace means to become a castaway, or rejected. But this is incorrect, as it really means that you leave God's unmerited, unearned, undeserved favour and go back under the Law and start to work and help God to realise your blessings. As Christians, we only have to believe God and His Word to experience His grace. Keeping the Law is 'deserved' favour; God's grace is 'undeserved' favour. However, it is important to understand that grace by itself is not enough for us to receive salvation, deliverance and everything else that Jesus died to give us. God has made 'all things' available by grace, but we need to exercise our faith to partake of everything Jesus' sacrifice provided. If grace alone was sufficient, every person on this earth would be partaking of Jesus' sacrifice and experiencing salvation, peace of mind, healing, and total prosperity; because God's grace for salvation has appeared to all men (Tit. 2:11). Grace and faith need to work together, and neither is sufficient on their own. Although living a righteous life, fasting, praying and obeying His command to love others as He loved us are important, what God provides by grace can only be received by faith, and not by any other way we may think of. Grace certainly cannot be accessed by works or performance (Eph. 2:7-8); in fact, grace and works cannot be blended (Rom. 11:6). In Paul's epistle to the Galatians, he warns that trying to earn grace by good works renders grace ineffective (Gal. 3:2-4), and says that it will result in us "falling from grace" (Gal. 5:4).

We please God when we humble ourselves and take a position to receive from Him. But as it is with our nature, we are not good receivers. When you give someone a gift, you often hear them say, 'Oh no, you should not have done this', or 'I do not deserve that'. We all need to ask God to make us better receivers, and to enlarge our capacity to receive not based on how deserving we think we are, but based solely on His grace to supply and give. Choose to see His loving heart, His undeserved favour toward you, and generous supply, and reach out in faith and take from God.

Chapter 4

Hindrances to Faith

4.1 Introduction

Believers are called to fight the good fight of faith. Paul, writing to Timothy said "(F)ight the good fight of faith..." (1 Tim. 6:12). For that reason, if there is a fight associated with faith, then there must be enemies or hindrances to faith, or Paul would not have told Timothy to fight because if there were no enemies or hindrances to faith, there would be no need to fight. I have heard people say that they were going to fight Satan. But this has always been a confusing statement to me as I have never been able to understand why anyone would want to fight Satan when Jesus has already defeated the devil on our behalf. Jesus was our Substitute when He defeated Satan, death, hell, and the grave through His redemptive work! In Rev. 1:18 Jesus tells John that He has "...the keys of Hades and of Death".

Having read to this point in the book, I trust that you are realising that faith is simply the hand that takes from the hand of God. We please God when we humble ourselves and take a position to receive from Him. By doing this we are allowing God to be Abba Father in our lives and He desires that. The Bible says that the lesser is always blessed by the greater (Heb. 7:7). But if these truths have not taken hold in your heart, the devil will try to steal this away from you, and the Lord wants you to be fully prepared for any situation or circumstance that may arise from Satan's deceit. Consequently, there are several obstacles that can prevent you attaining the highest kind of faith, being the faith which takes God at His Word and gets results. Many Christians become despondent when, after having learnt and put into practice the mechanics of Christianity, and all the right-to-do things, the fruits of the Christian lifestyle neither materialise, nor do they receive what God has made available to them by faith. As Christians we need to be aware of these obstacles to faith and actively resist them.

4.2 Our transformation through Christ

The first obstruction to faith is not having an appreciation of what it means, or a lack of understanding of what it comprises, to be a new creation in Christ; which can get in the way of a believer's faith lifestyle. 2 Cor. 5:17 says "Therefore, if anyone is in Christ, he is a new creation; old things have passed away; behold, all things have become new". Many Christians do not know what all is entailed in being a new creation. But 2 Cor. 5:17 is a key scripture that explains many other scriptures within the Bible. The Bible presents salvation as a life-transforming experience, with change being one of the distinguishing characteristics of true believers; yet many Christians think that God, through salvation, merely forgave them of their sins. For that reason, failure to understand that being made a new creation first takes place in your spirit, and then is reflected in your outward by way of thoughts and actions that are proportional to the way your mind is renewed (Rom. 12:2), has caused much confusion. As a born-again believer, you have been delivered from the power of darkness and from the authority of Satan through the blood of Jesus Christ (1 Pet. 1:19). We have been made God's own through the precious blood of Jesus. You have to know that by virtue of the new birth, you have been brought into the kingdom of Jesus Christ (Col. 1:13). You have to stand your ground against the enemy with your confession of faith in God's Word, because Satan is the god of this world and he will continue trying to exercise his authority over you in this life to regain authority over you. In Christ you have redemption through His blood, and you can overcome the devil in every fight, no matter what the test or trial is. Through the blood of the Lamb and your confession of faith (Rev. 12:11), you are more than a conqueror!

2 Cor. 5:17 describes this change, being salvation, as a total and complete (all things are become new, not just some things) experience; taking place in your born-again spirit (John 3:3). Your body does not display any change. Hence, if you were overweight before you were saved, you will still be overweight after you become saved. The new creation that Paul was speaking about is described in the following ways in Scripture: the new birth (John 1:13; John 3:3), the new creation (Gal. 6:15), His workmanship created in Christ Jesus (Eph. 2:10), newness of life (Rom. 6:4), a spiritual quickening (Eph. 2:1, 5), a spiritual resurrection (Col. 2:12; Col. 3:1), a new heart and spirit (Ezek. 36:26; Rom. 7:6), the putting on of the new man (Eph. 4:24), the inward man (Rom. 7:22), the circumcised heart (Rom. 2:29), the divine nature (2 Pet. 1:4), and restoration (Tit. 3:5). The new creation experience produces righteousness and true holiness (Gal. 5:24; Eph. 4:24; 1 John 2:29), conformance to the image of God's Son (Rom. 8:29), a heart that knows God (Jer. 24:7; Heb. 8:11), a hatred for sin and a love for righteousness (Isa. 59:2; Acts 3:19; 1 John 1:7; 1 John 3:7-10), good fruit yielded to God (Rom. 7:4), love for one another (1 John 4:7), and an active faith in Christ (1 John 5:1). Therefore, as believers, we are not just forgiven sinners. We are children of God, heirs of God and joint heirs with Jesus Christ (Rom. 8:17). Many people do not know they have eternal life. In his first epistle, John stated "These things I have written to you who believe in the name of the Son of God, that you may know that you have eternal life..." (1 John 5:13). When you know what you have and who you are in Christ, it makes all the difference in the world. We need to take notice of these things in the light of God's Word and in order to steadfastly resist any of Satan's attacks. Col. 1:12 says "...giving thanks to the Father who has qualified us to be partakers of the inheritance of the saints in the light". Preservation, healing, wholeness and prosperity are all part of our inheritance as children of God as we walk in the light.

The Bible tells us that we have dominion and authority over the devil through the blood of Jesus (Matt. 8:17; John 10:10; 1 Pet. 2:24). Thank God that we can partake of our inheritance right now, and do not need to wait until we get to heaven, because "...as He is, so are we in this world" (1 John 4:7). We have an inheritance now. We are delivered from the authority and power of darkness now. We are translated into the Kingdom of Jesus now. We have deliverance and redemption from the hand of Satan now. We can overcome the enemy now by the blood of the Lamb and by the word of our confession. We can glorify God now in our bodies and in our spirits which are God's now.

4.3 Our identity in Christ

The second obstruction to faith is not having an understanding of our place in Christ, and similarly, not having an understanding of Christ's place in our lives. By identification with Christ I am referring to an intimate relationship or union with Christ through His redemptive work. 2 Cor. 5:17 says "Therefore, if anyone is in Christ, he is a new creation; old things have passed away; behold, all things have become new". A study of the New Testament reveals expressions such as, 'in Christ', 'in whom', and 'in Him'. Everyone who identifies with Jesus Christ must become identified with Him in every phase of His life, namely His death, burial, resurrection, ascension and glorification. Once that takes place, you become a new creation. The life of Christ is reproduced in the child of God by the power of the Holy Spirit. Therefore, it is a new life with new relationships. It has a new source that is Jesus Christ. The Apostle Paul wrote "Christ who is our life..." (Col. 3:4). Jesus told His disciples, "I am the vine, you are the branches... abides in Me, and I in him..." (John 15:5). This transformation does not however take place in the physical realm, in our physical bodies, but rather in our spirit, or inward man, which is independent of our head and body. This is verified in 1 Thes. 5:23, where Paul is praying for the Thessalonians: "Now may the God of peace Himself sanctify you completely; and may your whole **spirit, soul**, and **body** be preserved blameless at the coming of our Lord Jesus Christ" (emphasis mine). This verse shows that we have a spirit, soul, and body, which I explained in Chapter 1. But to re-emphasise: the body is the part of us that can be seen, our outward person. Our soul comprises our emotional, mental part; which is also referred to as our mind/head. Then, according to Scripture, there is another part, which is our spirit. The spirit is the part of us that is changed and is new after salvation. Jas. 2:26 says "For as the body without the spirit is dead, so faith without works is dead also", and therefore confirms that it is the spirit that actually breathes life into our physical bodies. The word 'breathe' mentioned in Gen. 2 when God breathed into Adam the breath of life, in Hebrew is the exact same word that we use for breath (*nâphach*), and is even translated 'spirit' in other scriptures of the Bible. From Rom. 8:29 we discover that God's intention for His believers is the conformity of their character to the likeness of Christ. Everything that God does in our lives happens to focus on that one absolute purpose. God has selected beforehand the purpose that everyone who believes on Christ will be conformed to His likeness. God's primary concern is our character, functioning the way He intended us to function, and that being like Christ.

We are born physically with a spirit, soul, and body; but when we are born-again, we receive the Spirit of Christ. The very moment we believe on Christ as our personal Saviour we are baptised by the Holy Spirit, and we are placed into the Body of Christ. Gal. 4:6 says, "And because you are sons, God has sent forth the Spirit of His Son into your hearts, crying out, "Abba, Father!". God literally places His Spirit inside us, and our born-again spirit receives the full presence of God. Being members of the Body of Christ means that everything applicable to the Head is also applicable to every member of His Body (1 Cor. 12:13).

There is no lack or inadequacy in our spirit, but we have to realise that; which is why studying the Word of God is crucial to the Christian life. You are a totally brand-new person, but until you get knowledge, you will not change. Victory in the Christian life comes when you are able to look into the Word, which is Spirit and life, see who you are, see what God has done, and begin to believe it. Eph. 4:24 says "...put on the new man which was created according to God, in true righteousness and holiness". When a person is born-again, their spirit becomes righteous and holy. The Bible actually speaks of two types of righteousness. There is a righteousness you produce through your own actions, and you must maintain that type of righteousness in relationships with others (for example, adhering to the laws of the country that you reside in, obeying the policies and standards of your employer, showing consideration for your family and friends, etc.). God, however, does not accept you based on your external righteousness, and therefore the second type of righteousness is what we received of God by faith in Christ, which goes far beyond our external righteousness and is based on what God did for us. Eph. 2:10 confirms that in our spirits, we are perfect and complete. There is no sin or inadequacy. When a Christian sins, (s)he may feel that they have failed God, but this sense of guilt is related to their actions and their mental and emotional parts only; their spirit did not sin. God has sealed us, and for that reason when you were born-again, you received a new spirit, and sin cannot penetrate your spirit. You have a new identity. For you to have a relationship with God, you have to fellowship with Him and worship Him, based on who you are in your spirit and not in your flesh. This is the great transformation in the Christian life; that a person has to change their identity. You have to relate to God based not on what you do in the physical realm, not what you think in your mind, but by who you are in the spirit based on what He has done for you. You have to stand in this identity of who you are in Christ.

4.4 Right in the sight of God

The next obstruction to faith is not having an appreciation of what Jesus has done for us by faith (Rom. 5:17-18), and our attempts to be justified in the sight of God. The word 'righteousness' (and its matching part 'righteous') appear more times in the Bible than the word 'faith'; indicating that righteousness is important to understand. A lack of understanding, or an inaccurate understanding of how we become right in the sight of God, holds more Christians in bondage than anything else. Reading Psa. 32, "Blessed is he whose transgression is forgiven, whose sin is covered. Blessed is the man to whom the Lord does not impute iniquity..." (Psa. 32:1-2), you will notice that God attributed righteousness to those in the Old Testament whose sins had been covered by the blood of bulls and goats. Then, in 2 Cor. 5:21 we read "For He made Him who knew no sin to be sin for us, that we might become the righteousness of God in Him"; meaning that the New Covenant of grace and Jesus' finished work, the blood of Jesus, has cleansed us from all sin and through the new birth we have been made righteous. Righteousness is the condition of being in right relationship with the Lord, and can only happen through complete faith and dependence on Christ. There is no other way, and there is nothing we can add to our faith to obtain a right relationship with the Lord (Rom. 11:6). There is also a correlation between our actions and our right standing with God, but the direction of this correlation starts with our relationship with God which produces our actions, and not the other way around (in other words, we are not made righteous by what we do). Righteousness is a gift that comes from the Lord to those who accept what Jesus has done for them by faith (Rom. 5:17-18), thereby permitting us to stand in the presence of God without any sense of embarrassment, guilt, or condemnation.

The gift of salvation produces a changed heart that, in turn, changes our actions. Actions cannot change our hearts; and it is the heart of man that God looks upon (1 Sam. 16:7). The mistake of thinking that doing right makes us right is the same error the Pharisees made, and Jesus taught just the opposite (Matt. 23:25-26). Again, when a Christian sins (s)he experiences a sense of guilt, and then starts thinking that they are unworthy, or unrighteousness. They feel embarrassed and spiritually inferior to come into God's presence. But when we were born-again, our sins were remitted; and therefore we can come into the presence of God because we belong there. God said that He will not remember our sins (Isa. 43:25). Consequently, if God does not remember them, why should we? Someone may say (s)he has sinned since being born-again, but the good news is, according to Rom. 5:20 that "...where sin abounded, grace abounded much more". Smith Wigglesworth told of a time in England when an Episcopal minister, who was eighty years of age, asked him if he would come and pray for him because he wanted to receive the Holy Spirit. Wigglesworth told the man that God was not interested in beautiful prayers; but in faith alone. As they were praying (Wigglesworth said afterwards that he had never heard a more beautiful prayer than the one he heard that man pray), the elderly gentleman said 'God make me holy'. That elderly gentleman thought that before he could receive the Holy Spirit he had to be made holy. Wigglesworth then began to explain to him that he was already holy because he was a believer, and that the blood of Jesus had cleansed him from all sin. No sooner had Wigglesworth said that when the elderly man began to speak in tongues. That elderly gentleman did not have to do anything else in addition to being born-again in order to receive the infilling of the Holy Spirit. When we know that we are the righteousness of God in Christ, then we step out of the narrow place of failure and weakness where we have lived, and into the boundless fullness of God.

The wonderful plan of salvation is that those who put their faith in Jesus and what He did for us get what He deserves. On the other hand, those who do not put their total faith in Christ will ultimately get what they deserve. Jesus, as the Son of God, was in right relationship with God. He is God manifest in the flesh (1 Tim. 3:16). He is holy and pure and without sin, yet He became sin for us (2 Cor. 5:21), through no wrongdoing on His part. He took our sin in His own body on the cross (1 Pet. 2:24). "Surely He has borne our griefs and carried our sorrows; Yet we esteemed Him stricken, smitten by God, and afflicted. But He was wounded for our transgressions, He was bruised for our iniquities; The chastisement for our peace was upon Him, and by His stripes we are healed" (Isa. 53:4-5). In return for Jesus taking our sin, those who put their faith in Him get His righteousness instead of their own. It is not our actions that make us acceptable to the Father. Our righteousness is as filthy rags compared to God's righteousness (Isa. 64:6). It is our trust in Jesus that imparts His righteousness into our born-again spirits that makes us in right standing with God. Those who do not understand this righteousness, which comes from God as a gift, become frustrated trying to establish their own righteousness through good works (Rom. 10:3). We must trust completely in what Jesus did for us to obtain right relationship with God. Any trust in our own goodness will void the atonement Christ made for us (Gal. 5:4). Failure to understand this truth is at the root of all guilt and condemnation. Satan's only inroad into our lives is sin. If we understand our right standing with God on the basis of what Jesus did for us, and not by our own actions, then Satan's power to condemn is gone. Those who live with a feeling of unworthiness, or unrighteousness, are not trusting in God's righteousness but are looking to their own actions to obtain right standing with God. That will never work.

4.5 Using the name of the Lord Jesus Christ

The following hindrance to faith is not having an understanding of our privilege and right to use the Name of the Lord Jesus

Christ, and thereby not recognising that through His Name we have authority and power in this world today, empowering us to take our rightful position of authority over Satan and enjoy the victory in our lives that Jesus provided. God is the creator of all authority and power. When He created mankind, He gave them dominion over the earth (Gen. 1:26-28). God gave us authority and power to rule over this world, without any restrictions thereon. Authority is a right conferred by recognised social position. Authority often refers to power vested in an individual by a superior, and in general is the power, privilege, or influence over another of inferior rank or position. God gave Adam and Eve an unconditional, with no reservations or qualifications, authority over the earth (Psa. 82:6), something that He had never given to the angels. Lucifer saw this as an opportunity to rebel against God and advance his position above 'the anointed Cherub who covers' on God's holy mountain (Ezek. 28:14), and thereby become the new 'god' of this world (2 Cor. 4:4). Isaiah 14 reveals his consideration for this opportunity (Isa. 14:12-14). Lucifer saw how God gave Adam and Eve an unconditional authority; and even thought the Bible had not been written at this time, Lucifer knew that the Word of God was settled from the beginning (Psa. 119:89), and that the Lord never changes (Mal. 3:6). Therefore he knew that if mankind, of their own free will would yield to him, they would transfer that unconditional authority to him. As a result, he entered into a snake and used this serpent to speak to Eve and tempt her. Then he persuaded both Eve and Adam to eat of the forbidden fruit, and in so doing they yielded their authority to Satan, thereby making him the god of this world! As born-again believers, Jesus has restored that authority and power God gave to mankind, and much more. After Christ Jesus rose from the dead, He had authority in heaven, authority on earth, and authority under the earth (Phil. 2:10). After Jesus' resurrection, and before His ascension, He said to His disciples "All authority has been given to Me in heaven and on earth. Go therefore and make disciples of all the nations, baptizing them in the name of the Father and of the Son and of the Holy Spirit, teaching them to observe all things that I have commanded you; and lo, I am with you always, even to the end of the age..." (Matt. 28:18-20). The authority we have as believers in Christ Jesus today is superior to the authority Adam and Eve had. Jesus has reclaimed all authority and power lost, as well as authority over the demonic realm (Matt.10:1, 7-8). By the way, 'Christ' (or *Khristós* in the Greek) means 'anointed', and was used as a title for Jesus during His earthly ministry, therefore Jesus Christ/the Anointed. However, after Jesus' resurrection and ascension, and through His finished work on the cross, this title became part of His name, and He therefore became known as Christ Jesus, or the Anointed Jesus (Acts 19:4; Rom. 3:24; 1 Cor. 1:2).

Most Christians understand that the Name of Jesus can be used in prayer because of what Jesus said in John 16:23-24 and in Mark 16:15-18. However, many Christians are not using their God-given authority and power, and are allowing Satan to steal from them through sickness, disease, poverty, tragedy, or similar whilst confronting God and pleading with Him to intervene on their behalf. But God cannot intervene in your life if you are passive, as this negates His will and power in your life (Jas. 4:7). The Bible clearly mentions that we have "...power and authority over all demons..." (Luke 9:1). Many Christians do not realise that Satan is dominating their lives. They think that the adversity they are suffering is due to circumstances or fate. The Bible says "And you He made alive, who were dead in trespasses and sins, in which you once walked according to the course of this world, according to the prince of the power of the air, the spirit who now works in the sons of disobedience, among whom also we all once conducted ourselves in the lusts of our flesh, fulfilling the desires of the flesh and of the mind, and were by nature children of wrath, just as the others" (Eph. 2:1-3). Before our spirits were born-again, we were by nature children of Satan. He exerted power and influence over our lives. 2 Cor. 4:4 further states "...whose minds the god of this age has blinded, who do not believe, lest the light of the gospel of the glory of Christ, who is the image of God, should shine on them". The devil is actively at work today, hardening people and blinding them from the truths of the Gospel. This is not a passive battle; he is aggressively pursuing and trying to destroy people. One of the reasons why Satan has such a stronghold on so many people today is because the Church has not recognised the spiritual battle we are in (Eph. 6:12). For that reason, many Christians choose not to believe that there is an intense spiritual battle happening right now, but whether they do or not, the fact is that it is taking place. Their unwillingness to engage in battle does not mean that the battle is not taking place; it just means that they are being influenced, controlled and used by the devil. The release of God's power in your life is directly proportional to how you believe, and not proportional to your performance and good works. All of us come short, and the issue is faith. You get what you believe. If you believe that God has already healed you and you begin to exercise your authority, you will see that healing manifest. But if you believe that God can heal but He has not done it yet, then that healing will not transpire. Because of Christ's humility and obedience, God has given Him a name that is above every name in heaven, in earth, and under the earth (Phil. 2:9-10). If you can put a name to it, Jesus is above that. Sickness, poverty, depression, anger... everything has to bow its knee to the Lordship of Jesus. There is no exemption for anyone or anything from coming under the Lordship of Jesus. He is Lord of all.

4.6 Applying God's Word

In my opinion, the fifth impediment to faith is not realising the authority and capability within God's Word. One of the most amazing truths in the Bible is that God spoke into existence everything that we can see and beyond into the vast reaches of outer space. It is totally incredible that God made everything, from the grass we walk on to the stars in the night sky, by simply speaking them into existence.... It is therefore evident that nothing can stand in the way of God's words. There is no force in the universe that can refute, come against, or deny the power in God's overwhelming and unassailable Word. The Bible is God's Word, and none of His Word is void of power or impossible of fulfilment. Psa. 33:6 and 9 says "By the word of the Lord the heavens were made... For He spoke, and it was done". The Bible says that God's voice literally shook the mountain of Sinai when He spoke (Exod. 19:18). Paul also referred to this occurrence in Heb. 12:26 where it states "...whose voice then shook the earth...". God's Word cannot be opposed. It overcomes and conquers all that it is sent forth to defeat. Neither is there a circumstance that God's Word cannot prevail over; nor is there a problem in your life that God's Word cannot surmount. The Scripture declares that even the very pillars of heaven tremble at the words that God speaks (Job 26:11). Therefore, we need to learn to speak God's Word, as all our needs and desires can be supplied and satisfied through the Word of God. Psa. 12:6 declares that "The words of the Lord are pure words, like silver tried in a furnace of earth, purified seven times". Likewise, in 2 Cor. 1:20 we are assured that "...all the promises of God in Him are Yes, and in Him Amen, to the glory of God through us". Also, God promises us in Phil. 4:19 that He "...shall supply all your need according to His riches in glory by Christ Jesus". In Matt. 6:22 we are given the promise that if the eye is single, we will be full of light; meaning that if all your attention is focused on God through His Word, then the only thing that you will be full of is God and what His Word produces.

As Jesus maintained the anointing that was on His life and ministry by constantly abiding in the Father's presence, we are to continually recharge ourselves through prayer and meditation (Psa. 1:2; Jude 1:20). Many Christians neglect to keep in close enough communication and fellowship with God. Consequently, their prayers become ineffective and their words seem powerless. But the anointing of God never leaves us, because He promised to never leave us nor forsake us (Heb. 13:5). In order to be used mightily of God, we must keep on fire the anointing of God in our lives; and we do this by meditating on the Word of God and by living a life of prayer and dedication to God. We meditate on the Word of God by taking hold of the verse that has significance for us, memorise it and then begin to mutter it under our breath; and as we go about with a daily routine, we should regurgitate that verse and mutter it under our breath. Let us take Rom. 8:27 as an example of what I mean with meditating on the Word: "Yet in all these things we are more than conquerors through Him who loved us".

The way in which I meditate is by muttering and repeating to myself: in all things... everything being considered... all things considered..., then once I feel that my mind understands and has aligned itself with the Word of God, I move onto the next section of the verse: we are more than conquerors... I am victorious... all the spoils of war belong to me... I am victorious and Jesus fought and won this battle for... all I have to do is receive the benefits of being more than a conqueror..., and so I will continue until I have worked through the verse and as I said before, until once I feel that my mind understands and has aligned itself with the Word of God. Once your mind begins to understand and aligns itself with the Word of God, your spirit and soul (namely our personality, being our mind, our will, our emotions, and our conscience) will connect and a supernatural flow of the life of God from our spirit into our soul will take place. Meditating day and night on God's Word is the key to thriving, flourishing and seeing the blessing of God in all that we set our hands to do. Begin to experience greater health, peace, stability and unceasing fruitfulness as you meditate on the Lord's wonderful promises for you!

4.7 Our confession of faith

The last obstruction to faith that I would like to mention is not having an understanding that we are to hold fast to our confession of faith. In Heb. 10:23 it says "Let us hold fast the confession of our hope without wavering, for He who promised is faithful". In the Greek the word 'confession' is *homologeó* (Strong's Expanded Exhaustive Concordance, Greek Dictionary Number: 3670), and it means I confess, profess, acknowledge, praise. Faith is measured by our confession, and keeps pace with our confession. Rom. 10:10 states "For with the heart one believes unto righteousness, and with the mouth confession is made unto salvation". Sooner or later, we become what we confess. There are times when we just feel like speaking out our negative thoughts and emotions, as psychology today tells us that it is unhealthy to bury negative feelings. However, in light of the spiritual battle, we need to exercise our faith, as this battle is being fought in our minds, and not against flesh and blood; and it is only with faith that we are meant to overcome Satan's 'strongholds' and "Fight the good fight of faith..." (1 Tim. 6:12). In Matt. 6:31 Jesus states "...take no thought, saying..." (KJV). Therefore, a thought becomes your own when you speak it out of your mouth. You cannot keep thoughts from entering your mind. Kenneth E. Hagin used to say 'you cannot keep a bird from flying over your head, but you can keep it from landing there and building a nest'. Negative thoughts will come at times, but you have a choice. You do not have to entertain them. Negative thoughts and emotions do not have to become a part of you. If you do not voice them, they will not be yours. There is a confession of our hearts (the inward man, or the spirit) and a confession of our mouths (the soul, or the mind/head), and when these two synchronise, we become mighty in our Christian faith lifestyle. The reason so many Christians are defeated is that they have a negative confession. They talk of their weaknesses and failures and invariably this negative talk forms part of their confession. In

Mark 11:23 Jesus said "...he will have whatever he says". Our words enforce God's spiritual law that we are what we say. The choices you make, the things you say, the actions you take, and what you believe about what is happening around you determines whether God or Satan dominates in your life. This spiritual battle is for your heart and the hearts of every other person on earth. God is trying to influence people and draw them toward righteousness and toward Himself, to live consistent with Him so that His blessings can manifest in their lives. Satan, on the other hand, is waging all-out war trying to steal the hearts of people away from God. He wants to fill their hearts with his condemnation and corruption. But Satan cannot control you outside of your will. He cannot do anything without your cooperation and consent.

Many Christians do not realise that the words they speak have power, and we often speak them as though they are meaningless. Because of that, most Christians at one time or another have been hung by their tongue. You need to constantly be aware that your words are either releasing life or death. Do not allow just anything to come out of your mouth. Set a watch before your mouth and speak only life (Psa. 141:3), because you will eat the fruit of your tongue. Prov. 18:20 says "A man's stomach shall be satisfied from the fruit of his mouth; from the produce of his lips he shall be filled". Every word you utter out of your mouth is a seed that produces after its kind. If you are moaning, complaining, and speaking out negativity, then that is the fruit you will reap in your life. You cannot keep a problem from happening, but you can keep the problem from dominating you by speaking out correct, positive, God-inspired words. In this spiritual battle, Satan takes advantage of the words we speak. "For by your words you will be justified, and by your words you will be condemned" (Matt. 12:37). Believers do not realise just how important their words are. They speak foolishness, doubt, unbelief, and other things that allow Satan to devour them because they lowered their guard. An illustration of the power of a positive confession of faith, which resulted in healing is recorded in Mark 5:28 and 34: "For she said, 'If only I may touch His clothes, I shall be made well'.... And He said to her, 'Daughter, your faith has made you well...'". This woman voiced her faith, the confession of her heart became harmonised with the confession of her mouth, and she received the manifestation of what she believed and spoke!

We have discussed six important limitations to our faith, and by recognising these obstructions and renewing our minds with the Word of God, we will cause our faith to grow and increase. Faith is a way of living; it is the God-kind of Christian lifestyle. Faith should not be something you use when you have a problem, or when you have a crisis, but rather faith ought to be your life characteristic. Every Christian can see the promises of God come to pass in his/her life when we will take time to meditate on who we are in Christ and what we have in Christ and act like God's Word is true (Heb. 11:6). The Bible confirms that God is a rewarder of them that diligently seek Him.

Chapter 5

In Times of Trouble

5.1 Introduction

One of the greatest mistakes many Christians make is to confess their faith in the Word of God and at the same time contradict their confession by wrong actions. We say that we are trusting God to provide for our financial needs, but at the same time we are worrying about how we are going to pay our debts. One minute we confess that the Word of God is true, and the very next moment we repudiate everything we say by wrong actions. Our actions have to correspond with our believing if we are to take from the hand of God by faith. The epistle of James was not writing to the unbelievers, but to believers. He said in Jas. 2:14-22 "What does it profit... faith by itself, if it does not have works, is dead...". He was writing to fellow Christians scattered throughout the world, highlighting that faith without corresponding actions will not work for them, even though they are believers. In addition, James warns the readers in Jas. 1:22 not to deceive themselves by blaming their problems on the devil or on something else when in reality they are not doers of the Word.

5.2 The storms of life

In the conclusion of Jesus' sermon to His disciples in Matt. 7:24-27, He gives an illustration of a storm that thrashed two houses. The rains, floods, and the winds came against both houses exactly the same, but the reason why the damage to the two houses was not identical was due to differences in the house's foundations. Everyone, even Christians, will have problems come their way (Acts 14:22; 2 Tit. 3:12), but those who are rooted and grounded in doing the Word of God will stand. The reason why one house was destroyed and the other was not destroyed is because the wise man was a doer of the Word and the foolish man was not. It is much harder to put a foundation in rock than in sand. This is a further explanation for Matt. 7:14 as to why few find the narrow way that leads to life. When the storms of life come, we all know of many Christians that feel the effects of these storms and are subsequently defeated. But it is not the storms that defeat them, for if it was these storms would defeat us all. Some Christians face a storm and are not defeated, while other Christians who face the same storm are destroyed. It is my opinion that those Christians who are not defeated are acting on God's Word. The defeated Christians may have knowledge and understanding of God's Word, yet their actions do not correspond with their faith as they exercise their faith by what they can see, hear and or feel. These defeated Christians are taking the path that demands the least effort, with no thought of the future. But doing the sayings of Jesus is the sure safeguard against self-deception. The storms of life will take the form of sickness, disease, poverty, tragedy or similar tragedies; but the Word is sound in its doctrine. The Christian that acts on his/her faith, being a doer of the Word, will set in motion God's power and (s)he will move those mountains in their lives.

The approach to making God's Word your own is to act on it. Do exactly what His Word says (Pro. 3:5). It is human nature to be concerned about the storms in our personal lives. Worry, feeling uneasy or troubled, plagues everyone, including Christians; but we need to be careful as the devil will cause us to worry beyond what is reasonable. Worry is like a carousel, it is always in motion but it never gets you anywhere. As I stated in a previous chapter, we learn to trust God by going through many experiences that require trust. The proof that we trust God is to refuse to worry. Worry is the opposite of faith, and it steals our peace, physically wears us out, and can even make us sick. When we worry, we torment ourselves and takeover and do the devil's job for him! Worry is caused by not trusting God to take care of the various situations in our lives. Too often we trust our own abilities, believing that we can figure out how to take care of our own problems. Yet sometimes, after all our worry and effort, we come up with solutions that are unsuitable to resolve the worry in our lives. Mistrust is a result of people hurting us. We try to take care of ourselves, with the mind-set that we will not depend on anyone. Unfortunately, in our Christian lifestyle we encounter these experiences, it takes a long time to overcome these feelings. As a result, we find it difficult to trust God, but we have to make the effort to trust in the Lord by trusting in His Word. You cannot trust in the Lord without trusting His Word. God and His Word are one, similar to the way that you and your word are one. If your word is not good, then you are not good. If God's Word is not good, then He is not good. But His Word is good and He watches over His Word. "Then the Lord said to me, 'You have seen well, for I am ready to perform My word' " (Jer. 1:12). If you do not take the Word to be yours, He does not have anything to make good in your life. As God's children, and New Covenant believers, we are fully entitled to partake of everything Jesus' sacrifice provided: salvation, peace of mind, healing, total prosperity, and much, much more... but you need to act on His Word.

Until there are corresponding actions, there will be continual failure in life. We can confess and say that God is our strength, but if at the same time we continue to talk about our weaknesses and lack of faith, we will be defeated because there is no corresponding action. Faith without corresponding actions is human reasoning, and not trusting the Lord. Our body and soul (mind/head) is our worst enemy. Our mind/head, which is not born-again with the new birth experience (Rom. 12:2), and natural human reasoning limit our abilities. We look to the circumstances, the problems, the trials and tests, and storms and say 'we can't'; but through faith we should be saying 'I can do all things through Christ who strengthens me' (Phil. 4:13). Paul never said that he could do all things because he was an apostle, equipped with special powers, or grace. He said "I can do all things through Christ...", and we have this same access to Christ. 2 Cor. 5:17 says "Therefore, if anyone is in Christ, he is a new creation; old things have passed away; behold, all things have become new". You are a new creation in Christ too; Christ does not belong to Paul any more than He belongs to you.

5.3 The fourth dimension

In the universe there are three types of spirits, namely: the Holy Spirit, the spirit of Satan, and the human spirit. In geometry when you place two dots on a sheet of paper and join these dots by drawing a line, this is called one dimension as it is considered to have length only. When you begin duplicating this line and placing it alongside the original line you drew, that one dimension now becomes two dimensions (also called a plane) as you now have length and breadth. Stacking multiple planes on one another creates a third dimension (called a cube) as you now have length, breadth and height. This earth is material, and is three dimensional. In mathematics, an inequality is a relation that holds between two values when they are different, and states that if the values in question are elements of an ordered set, they can be compared in size. For that reason, the second dimension (plane or flat surface) contains and controls the first dimension, and similarly the third dimension (cube) includes and therefore controls the second dimension. However, there is one higher dimension that controls the third dimension, and this is the fourth dimension. This dimension has been studied by mathematicians and philosophers for almost three hundred years, both for its own interest and for the insights it offered into mathematics and related fields. David Yonggi Cho in his book 'The Fourth Dimension' (1979) states that God gave him revelation knowledge that the spirit world is the fourth dimension, and this spiritual dimension controls our familiar three-dimensional world. Hence, the mechanics of faith operate in this fourth dimension.

Everyone, both believer and unbeliever, is both a spiritual and a physical being. We belong to the fourth dimension as well as the third dimension. David Yonggi Cho mentions in his book 'So men by operating in their spiritual area of the fourth dimension through developing concentrated visions and dreams in their imaginations can brood over and incubate the third dimension, influencing and changing it'. In the Bible, Luke mentioned this in Acts 2: 14-17 when he recorded Peter saying "...Men of Judea and all who dwell in Jerusalem, let this be known to you, and heed my words... this is what was spoken by the prophet Joel: 'And it shall come to pass in the last days, says God, that I will pour out of My Spirit on all flesh; your sons and your daughters shall prophesy, your young men shall **see visions**, your old men shall **dream dreams**. And on My menservants and on My maidservants I will pour out My Spirit in those days; and they shall prophesy...' " (emphasis mine). As we link our spirits that are residing in the fourth dimension through faith to the Holy Father, being the Creator of the universe, and who also has residence in the fourth dimension, we can exercise dominion over our circumstances. Praise God! Have you ever noticed how people practicing Yoga, and even Buddhists, are able to explore and develop their human fourth dimension, their spiritual sphere; and with clear-cut visions and mental pictures of health they can nurture their physical bodies. Remember the fourth dimension has power over the third dimension, and the human spirit, within limitations, has the power to give order and creation. God gave mankind dominion over the earth (Gen. 1:26-28), or said another way: God gave mankind power to control our three-dimensional world; and this dominion or power to control can be exerted from the fourth dimension. Christians should embrace this opportunity and develop their inner spiritual being to exercise dominion on their third dimension, which encloses sickness, disease, poverty, tragedy, or similar tragedies. This is how the magicians in Egypt performed various miracles similar to Moses (Exod. 7:22) by appropriating control over material things.

Your sub-conscious comprises the hidden person of the heart that Peter mentions in 1 Pet. 3:4. The sub-conscious is part of our inward man, or our heart of man, or our spirit; and therefore does operate in the fourth dimension, albeit with limited influences (we cannot create as God can). We must however bear in mind that the fourth dimension is always creating and giving order, whether good or bad; and therefore the devil also occupies this fourth dimension. Similar to the way a mother hen sits on her eggs to provide them with the required stimulus and incubation to promote maturation and development to eventually produce chicks, the Holy Spirit incubates the third dimension as does Satan. When we watch television programmes not suitable for Christians, we provide Satan with an inroad to our lives by incubating those wrong actions and or behaviours we see the actors and actresses performing. We are limited by space and time, and can only incubate and operate in the fourth dimension through our imagination, visions and dreams. God uses our sub-conscious to communicate with and guide us by His Spirit using imaginations, visions and dreams. Pro. 29:18 states that "Where there is no vision, the people perish..." (KJV). Visions and dreams are the language of the fourth dimension, and the Holy Spirit speaks through them. Only through a vision or a dream can you visualise spiritual growth and increase that need to be incubated to produce a result in the future. We can see this incubation process with Eve when she saw the fruit... "So when the woman saw that the tree was good for food, that it was pleasant to the eyes... she took of its fruit and ate..." (Gen. 3:6). I am certain that Eve saw herself eating the fruit, imagining what it would taste like, the inviting colour of its interior flesh, the fruit's natural juices.... If imagination, visions and dreams are not important then why did the angel instruct Lot's wife not to look back when they fled from Sodom (Gen. 19:17)? She looked back and received judgment for that action. In Gen. 13:14-15 we read about God instructing Abram to visualise the lands he was to possess. God did not say, 'Abram, if you name it, claim it, and blab it, I will give you Canaan'. Abram had to imagine, visualise and dream about the land he was to possess. Once Abram began using his sub-conscious and see the land he was to possess, the Holy Spirit began to incubate and influence this visualisation in the fourth dimension for it to materialise in our three-dimensional world. Again, like Eve, I am certain that Abram sat at the entrance of his tent, and looking out over the desert towards the Hebron hills which at that time was devoid of settlements, imagined possessing it all. Those images probably recurred in his thoughts and dreams regularly, and hence became part of his fourth dimension. Abram was now operating in the language of the fourth dimension, the language of spiritual visions and dreams. Those dreams and visions carried dominion over his physical body, and from that time onwards he believed the Word of God and he praised God. If Abram could use the mechanics of faith to operate in this fourth dimension to take possession of the land through developing a concentrated vision and dream of the land in his imagination, and brood over and incubate this vision and dream by using his sensory knowledge of the third dimension, and subsequently influence and change his three-dimensional world, then you too can operate in the fourth dimension.

God gave visions to Joseph, Isaiah, Jeremiah, Ezekiel and Daniel, all great servants of the Lord. God called them into the fourth dimension, and taught them the language of the Holy Spirit. There are approximately 350 promises in the Bible, all attainable through the fourth dimension. By reading Scripture you can learn of the victorious life God has for us, take in the language of the Holy Spirit, and allow the Holy Spirit to quicken the Scripture to you and make your dreams and visions a reality.

5.4 Faith contradicts circumstances

We can all allude to experiences where we did not believe that our prayers were answered. Unanswered prayers are a major obstacle that hinders our life of true faith, and results in us focusing on the symptoms, conditions, and the actual problems, crises or desires that caused us to pray in the first instance. But focusing on the wrong areas triggers unbelief and destroys the effects of our prayers. In Matt. 7:7 the Bible says, "Ask, and it will be given to you; seek, and you will find; knock, and it will be opened to you". Once you pray, you need to keep your mind focused on the answer to your prayer. See yourself as having received and constantly affirm, even in the face of contrary evidence, that God has heard your prayer because the Word says that He will never leave us nor forsake us (Heb. 13:5); and in Rom. 3:4 we are reassured "...let God be true but every man a liar...". The believing comes before the receiving. You have to believe you have received before you actually receive. Heart faith believes the Word of God; and to believe with the heart means to believe with your spirit, or inward man, which is independent of your physical senses. When we fail to believe, we do not experience the promises of God. In contrast, when we do believe, we allow God to use His power in and through us (Matt.17:20; Matt. 21:21; Luke 7:9-10). All things are possible to them that believe. 'I doubt that I can make it, but I hope I can. Pray for me that I will hold out faithfully to the end' is a familiar prayer request. But that is not what God told us to say. Too many Christians are boldly proclaiming that they are beaten and defeated, and being trodden on by Satan. But nowhere in the Bible do we find where God said to proclaim that. It is simply wrong thinking, wrong believing, and wrong talking that causes Christians to experience a sense of being trampled and defeated. Satan cannot defeat you as Jesus has already defeated him on your behalf. Satan does not defeat any Christian, we defeat ourselves. Or if he does overcome you, it is because you permit him to do so. God has given us His Word to direct us in our believing; and if our believing is correct, our thinking will be correct and this will promote correct talking. Kenneth E. Hagin cites a story of a man with a heavy pack on his back walking down the railroad track, and comes across a section gang repairing the railroad, and the foreman tells the man to get off the track, but the man shows him his valid railroad ticket. The foreman then expresses to the man that this railroad ticket does not give him the right to walk on the tracks. Hagin's analogy is that many Christians are like this man in that they are on the right track, but they are walking instead of riding. Also, they are carrying their own baggage when they have a valid railroad ticket that entitles them to have the railroad company carry the heavy load. The Bible says, "...casting all your care upon Him, for He cares for you" (1 Pet. 5:7). Pro. 4:20-22 says "...give attention to my words; Incline your ear to my sayings. Do not let them depart from your eyes; Keep them in the midst of your heart; For they are life to those who find them, and health to all their flesh". Verses 20 and 21 are the directions for experiencing the promises of God. Like medicine, the Word of God has to be taken as instructed in order for it to work.

We need to accept that the Bible is the actual Word of God, and to be taken literally, word for word. Therefore, if God has made provision for everyone to be healed (Psa. 103:3; Acts 10:38; 1 Pet. 2:24), then we are healed; If God has made financial provision for everyone (Deut. 28:8; Matt. 6:33; 2 Cor. 8:9; Phil. 4:19), then our needs are met and we are prosperous; and if He has made provision for everyone to be saved (1 Tim. 4:10; 2 Pet. 3:9; 1 John 2:2). In other words, once we truly believe in our hearts what God's Word says, we are well on the way to seeing what we believe materialise in the physical realm. We have what the Word says we have. We are what the Word says we are.

Because Jesus is our High Priest and sits at the right hand of God in heaven (Heb. 4:14), and making intercession for us (Rom. 8:34), we can have the answers to our petitions right now. As I mentioned in an earlier chapter, the word 'confession' in the Greek language is to speak the same, to agree. Jesus is in heaven, representing us at the throne of God. He did not die for Himself. He did not need to redeem Himself because He was lost. He died for us. He became our substitute; He took our sins; He bore our sicknesses and carried our diseases. He died for us, arose from the dead for us, and ascended on high for us. Jesus is beside our Abba Father (1 Tim. 2:5) making all that God is and has, available to us; and our responsibility is to speak what Jesus is speaking, and agree with what He is proclaiming over us! Faith, kept only in your heart, will never bring healing to your body or the infilling of the Holy Spirit, or even an answer to prayer. But faith in your heart, released through your mouth, will bring results. We are not to pray for more faith, but rather we are to ask, seek, and knock on behalf of the specific answers we desire (Matt. 7:7). In other words, we are to focus on the 'things hoped for', and when the answer comes then faith comes. Faith is the reality of what is hoped for, the proof of what is not seen. Faith is not vague or ambiguous; it is specific to that which you are asking and seeking. But, as I said before, the Word of God has to be taken as instructed in order for it to work.

If you cannot boldly speak your faith, then your faith will be too weak to move your mountain. The medical profession has led us to assume that the words we speak originate in our mind/head, but that is not always the case. The Bible says "...For out of the abundance of the heart his mouth speaks" (Luke 6:45). Whatever is in your heart will come out of your mouth, regardless of whether it is rage, resentment, fear, love, compassion or faith. Hence, if faith is not coming out of your mouth, then you are probably not in faith. You may think you are operating in faith, when in fact you may only be hoping and operating in belief; and only hoping and believing will not have any impact on your circumstances. James states that the mouth is one of the most difficult members to tame, but once it is tamed, the whole body will respond (Jas. 3:1-11). This can be likened to a tube of toothpaste; when the pressures of life squeeze you, what is on the inside will come out. If you want good things to come out, then you must put good things in. There is an old saying of 'garbage in, garbage out' that was coined by George Fuechsel as a teaching mantra for programmable computing devices, but this can be considered as worthy insight for all of us. This is the purpose for a good confession, as our confession of faith in God's Word will place His Word in our hearts and allow that seed to conceive, which will manifest what we believe and speak.

5.5 Continuing in faith

The highest level of faith is not to passively direct everything to God and then count on Him to do everything on our behalf. Some might say that this is the correct approach to adopt as it is in a sense submission to God. However, God desires active seeking and active obedience. His desire is for us to depend on Him in all that we do, and not for us to depend on Him to do it all. The impression of active obedience to God's will is not us sitting quietly in the back seat and allowing God to drive the car. Instead, it is us actually driving the car with God providing the directions. Driving the car does not amount to us 'grabbing the wheel' from God. He gave us the responsibility to drive the car, and we are to take personal accountability for the position God has (pre)determined for us. Active obedience is receiving instantaneous directions from the LORD, and using them to advance His plans for us. When we ask anything in prayer, God moves immediately and gives us the answer in our spirits. We are responsible for believing that, and acting accordingly by faith to bring the answer into the physical world. God is a Spirit (John

4:24), and He always answers back to our born-again spirit. Through faith, we then give physical substance (Heb. 11:1) to what God has done. In other words, we convert God's answers to our prayer into a physical reality through our actions. That is not to say that it is us who produces the answer by our own power, but rather it is God who works the miracle, and it is manifest through us. Eph. 3:20 says, "Now to Him who is able to do exceedingly abundantly above all that we ask or think, **according to the power that works in us**" (emphasis mine).

Faith is the only active ingredient in prayer. Prayer on its own is just the container by which a specific faith gets communicated to God in exchange for a specific desired hope. The Word is sound in its doctrine, but when someone tries the Word and does not see the promised results, rather than admit that they could have failed, they say something like, 'that must have passed away with the apostles' or 'it must not have been God's will', etc. God is not the one who failed to answer, but rather we are the ones who have failed to receive. Now you can understand better what Mark 11:24 means when it says, "...whatever things you ask when you pray, believe that you receive them, and you will have them". You receive in your spirit by faith whatever things you ask immediately, and it manifests in the physical later. It may be one minute, one day, or one year; but you cannot waiver in your belief that God has already answered your prayer. The time that it takes for God's answer to be manifest in the physical is dependent on many things, but it is not God who determines that. God answers immediately. Remember, the scripture says that you must believe that you receive "when you pray". God is not asking you to believe something that is not true. You do receive instantly in your born-again spirit, but there is time before it is manifest in the physical. Faith is the currency, prayer is the transaction, and hope is the purchased object.

Chapter 6

God-kind of Faith

6.1 Introduction

Faith is the most important subject in the Bible, and one of the fundamentals of Christianity, yet the least taught by the Church today and therefore the least understood and exercised subject by Christians. You cannot be saved without faith, because "...by grace you have been saved through faith..." (Eph. 2:8), neither can you live without faith nor please God without faith, because the Bible says "For we walk by faith, not by sight" (2 Cor. 5:7), and "...without faith it is impossible to please Him..." (Heb. 11:6). "Grace and peace be multiplied to you in the knowledge of God and of Jesus our Lord, as His divine power has given to us all things that pertain to life and godliness, through the knowledge of Him who called us by glory and virtue, by which have been given to us exceedingly great and precious promises, that through these you may be partakers of the divine nature, having escaped the corruption that is in the world through lust" (2 Pet. 1:2-4). These verses say that all things that concern life and godliness are given to us through the knowledge of God. For that reason faith must be included in the 'all things' in order for Christians to experience the power and presence of God, and experience God at work in their lives; and this comes through the knowledge of God. That is the reason Rom. 10:17 says that faith comes by hearing the Word of Christ. The amount of faith that you operate in is directly proportional to the revelation knowledge that you have of God through His Word.

6.2 Operating in faith

Faith is our positive response to what God has already done for us. It is our response to His grace. It is not what we must do to make the Lord act on our behalf, but rather our response to what He has already done. In its simplicity, that is faith. As I mentioned in my opening chapter, there are two kinds of faith – the Thomas-like faith (or 'head' faith), and the Abraham-like faith (or 'heart' faith). The Thomas-like faith is inherent within every human being, whilst the Abraham-like faith is a supernatural faith that only comes to those who receive the Good News. After Jesus' resurrection, He appeared to the disciples, "Now Thomas... was not with them when Jesus came. The other disciples therefore said to him, 'We have seen the Lord'. So he said to them, 'Unless I see in His hands the print of the nails, and put my finger into the print of the nails, and put my hand into His side, I will not believe'" (John 20:24-25). Several days later, whilst the disciples were gathered together in a room, Jesus again appeared in their midst, and He said to Thomas, "...Reach your finger here, and look at My hands; and reach your hand here, and put it into My side. Do not be unbelieving, but believing" (John 20:27). Jesus knew what Thomas had said even though He was not physically present that day when Thomas said it. We read on in John 20:28 that Thomas acknowledged Jesus as "...My Lord and my God", and Jesus said to him, "...Thomas, because you have seen Me, you have believed. Blessed are those who have not seen and yet have believed" (John 20:29). Using 'head' faith, which God has given to every person, if I asked you to board an aeroplane that was missing one of its wings, your physical senses would forbid you to board that aeroplane even if you were offered bags of money to do so. In the same manner, Jesus did not commend Thomas' kind of faith. That is believing what your physical senses tell your mind; and everybody, believer and non-believer, has that kind of faith. Rather, Jesus applauded the Abraham-kind of faith, which believes in spite of what our physical senses can perceive, or our circumstances can portray (John 20:29).

Look at Rom. 4:17, it says, "...God... calls those things which do not exist as though they did". God's faith goes beyond our physical senses. God's faith operates supernaturally, beyond the limitations of our 'head' faith. The context of this verse from Romans speaks about how God supernaturally blessed Abram and Sarai with a child in their old age. Abram was 100 and Sarai was 91 when Isaac was born. Luke 18:27 reminds us that "...the things which are impossible with men are possible with God". The year before Isaac's birth, when Abram still did not have a child by his wife, God told them the child was coming, and He changed Abram's name to Abraham and Sarai's name to Sarah. Abram meant 'high father', but Abraham means 'to be populous, father of a multitude'. God changed Abram's name and called him the father of a multitude before it came to pass. God also changed Sarai's name by adding the same letter to her name that was added to Abram's name, being the Hebrew letter A (pronounced 'heh' or 'hey' and symbolises grace). The name Sarai signifies 'my princess', as if her honour were confined to one family only; but Sarah signifies a 'princess' of multitudes. Rom. 4:17 explains this action by stating that "...God... calls those things which do not exist as though they did". This supernatural faith is, as I mentioned before, also the kind of faith we use to receive salvation. We have to believe in God, whom we have not seen, and believe that our sins are forgiven, which we cannot prove by natural means. It takes God's supernatural faith for us to receive salvation, and this supernatural faith comes from God's Word. Rom. 10:17 says "So then faith comes by hearing, and hearing by the word of God". We access God's faith through His Word, and His Word always achieves that which it is meant to accomplish (Isa. 55:11). Once we receive God's supernatural faith at salvation, it does not leave us, according to Rom.11:29: "For the gifts and the calling of God are irrevocable". After we receive salvation however, we are to continue our personal relationship with God in Christ Jesus, using Abraham-like faith, and not revert to using Thomas-like faith! What God provides by grace can only be received by faith, and not by works or performance (Eph. 2:7-8).

6.3 Sovereignty of God

The Church today leads us to believe that God controls us, and manipulates us independent of our will, and that nothing can happen without His approval. The Church has expanded the word 'sovereign' to mean God controls everything, and that nothing can happen other than what He wills or allows. The dictionary does not define the word 'sovereign' as meaning a deity controlling everything, nor does the Bible translate and use the word 'sovereign' as meaning God controls everything. Rather, 'sovereign' means having supreme rank, power, or authority. In 2 Pet. 3:9, Peter said "The Lord is... not willing that any should perish but that all should come to repentance". God has made us accountable for our own lives, and it is our free will that damns us, not God. This scripture undoubtedly highlights God's will for people concerning salvation, yet people are still experiencing despair. In Matt. 7:13 Jesus said, "Enter by the narrow gate; for wide is the gate and broad is the way that leads to destruction, and there are many who go in by it". God does not desire anyone to perish, but the Lord gave us the freedom to choose. He paid for the sins of the whole world (1 John 2:2; 1 Tim. 4:10), but we must choose to put our faith in Christ and receive His salvation.

God gave us dominion over the earth (Gen. 1:28), but mankind surrendered that dominion and power to Satan through his deceitful act in the Garden of Eden. As a result, Jesus was spoken into existence as the Son of Man to regain dominion and power on the earth, and restore mankind to their rightful position. Jesus made us co-heirs with Him, but God still cannot do anything on this earth without our cooperation. In Eph. 3:20 we can see this point made clear as it states "...according to the power that works in us". Wrong thinking about the sovereignty of God is one of the biggest problems people have in exercising their faith. If you believe God is the One who is causing all the problems in the world, it will definitely affect your relationship with Him. Jesus clearly stated that He did not come to destroy men's lives, but to save them (Luke 9:56). This was said in response to His disciples wanting to call fire down from heaven on the Samaritans as judgment, just as Elijah had done in the Old Testament. Yet it is written in our insurance contracts that major natural disasters and tragedies are "acts of God".... There is a future time described in the book of Revelation, when God's judgment will be released on the whole world, and no one will have to be told that it is God. The people will cry out for the rocks to fall on them and hide them from the wrath of God (Rev. 6:12-17); but that time has not come, we are still living in an age of grace where God is not imputing men's sins to them (2 Cor. 5:19). God does not directly control the events on earth; He is not the source of our problems. God has a good plan for us, but that plan has to have our cooperation in order to come to pass and we need to realise that any problems in our lives are from the devil (Rom. 6:16), or from our own choices, or just as a result of living in a fallen world. Understanding the sovereignty of God correctly is so important, and anyone who does not get a grasp of this will overlook forming an intimate relationship or union with Him in Jesus Christ, being the objective of our faith! It is impossible to feel good about God if you believe the accusers that depict Him as being evil.

6.4 Have faith in God

In Mark 11, after Jesus transformed a fig tree in full bloom to a shrivelled remnant, He told His disciples to have "...faith in God" (Mark 11:22) Many people suggest that this verse should read, 'have the God-kind of faith'. While it is certainly true that New Testament believers are given a God-kind of faith and not just a natural human faith, the vast majority of scholars and translations agree that this verse is correctly stressing having faith in God. We use this God-given, God-kind of faith, but it must always be put in the Lord and not in our actions, abilities, or even our God-given faith. In verse 23 Jesus went on to explain what "...faith in God" meant, being that it is the kind of faith in which a believer trusts with his/her heart and says with his/her mouth that which (s)he believes in his/her heart, and it takes place. Jesus demonstrated that He had that kind of faith, for He believed that what He said would happen. He said to the fig tree, "...Let no one eat fruit from you ever again" (Mark 11:14). This is the kind of faith that spoke the world into existence. "By faith we understand that the worlds were framed by the word of God, so that the things which are seen were not made of things which are visible" (Heb. 11:3). God believed that what He said would happen. He spoke the Word and there was an earth. He spoke into existence the solar system, vegetation, wildlife and humankind. He said it and it was so. That is the God-kind of faith: God believed what He said would happen and it did. Jesus demonstrated the God-kind of faith to His disciples, and then He told them that they too had that kind of faith, to believe with the heart and say with the mouth or confess what is believed.

When you compare Rom. 10:8 to Mark 11:23, it is obvious that Paul's writings to the Christians in Rome agree exactly with what Jesus told His disciples when He said, "...whoever says... and does not doubt in his heart, but believes... he will have whatever he says". We see here the basic principle that is essential to the God-kind of faith: believing with the heart and speaking with the mouth. Jesus believed it and He said it. God believed it and He said it, we need to believe and speak out.... Many times, when Christians are asked when they were saved, they often respond by saying something like, 'about 7pm on the 30th of January'. But this is incorrect as God saved them nearly two thousand years ago. It only became a reality to them when they believed it and confessed it (Rom. 10:9-10). Salvation belongs to everyone. Jesus died for the whole world, not just for you and me. Every man and woman in this world has a legal right to salvation, and a measure of faith is dealt to them through hearing the Word. When a sinner hears the Good News, it causes faith to come. When (s)he believes and confesses, the reality of his/her salvation is created in his/her own life by faith. Just as faith comes from hearing the Word of Christ, so does anything else that we receive from God. God causes the God-kind of faith to come into the hearts of those who hear. It is therefore of no surprise that Jesus said "Therefore take heed how you hear..." (Luke 8:18). You cannot let the Word of Christ go in one ear and out the other, this will be of no benefit to you as this will not yield any faith. It is only when you are devoted to receiving the Word of Christ, and sincerely accept it, that when you act on the Word then your actions will produce faith.

The key to exercise our God-kind of faith is by believing with the heart and confessing with the mouth. Every word you utter out of your mouth is a seed that produces after its kind: they can render us victors or keep us captives. We can fill our words with faith or we can fill our words with doubt. Our words either encourage and edify, or contaminate and demolish; and our faith will never rise above our words. For example, the words spoken to a child as (s)he leaves for school in the morning will impact on that child's success or failure during the day. If you are constantly telling a child that they are a failure and that they will never succeed in anything they do, those words will stay with them and bear fruit in their life. Similarly, kind words spoken to your partner or spouse in the morning can contribute to a sense of well-being as those words edify and build-up the hearer of those words.

Negative thoughts will come but they do not have to shape you, you have a choice. Satan offers wrong thinking to everyone, but as Christians we do not have to accept his offer. Jesus referred to him as "...the devil... there is no truth in him... he is a liar and the father of it" (John 8:44). The Bible provides many detailed instructions on what we are to think about, namely that which will build us up and not tear us down. Our thoughts affect our attitudes; for that reason we need to learn to use words that will react to our spirits. As our confessions of faith precede our possessions, we need to be thoughtful of the words we speak.

RECEIVE JESUS AS YOUR SAVIOUR

Choosing to receive Jesus Christ as your Lord and Saviour is the most important decision you will ever make!

God's Word promises, "...that if you confess with your mouth the Lord Jesus and believe in your heart that God has raised Him from the dead, you will be saved. For with the heart one believes unto righteousness, and with the mouth confession is made unto salvation.... For "whoever calls on the name of the Lord shall be saved" (Rom. 10:9–10, 13).

By His grace, God has already done everything to provide salvation. Your part is simply to believe and receive. Pray out loud:

Jesus, I confess that You are my Lord and Saviour. I believe in my heart that God raised You from the dead. By faith in Your Word, I receive salvation now. Thank You for saving me!

The very moment you commit your life to Jesus Christ, the truth of His Word instantly comes to pass in your now born-again spirit. You are now a brand-new you!

RECEIVE THE HOLY SPIRIT

As His child, your heavenly Father wants to give you the supernatural power you need to live this new life.

The Bible says "For everyone who asks receives, and he who seeks finds, and to him who knocks it will be opened.... If you then... know how to give good gifts to your children, how much more will your heavenly Father give the Holy Spirit to those who ask Him!" (Luke 11:10, 13). All you have to do is ask, believe, and receive! Pray out loud:

> Father, I recognise my need for Your power to live this new life. Please fill me with Your Holy Spirit. By faith, I receive Him right now! Thank You for baptising me. Holy Spirit, You are welcome in my life.

Congratulations! You are filled with God's supernatural power. Some syllables from a language you do not recognise will rise up from your heart to your mouth. (1 Cor. 14:14). As you speak them out loud by faith, you will be releasing God's power from within and building yourself up in the Spirit (1 Cor. 14:4). You can do this whenever and wherever you like.

It does not matter whether you felt anything or not when you prayed to receive the Lord and His Spirit. If you believe in your heart that you received, then God's Word promises you did. According to Mark 11:24 which says "Therefore I say to you, whatever things you ask when you pray, believe that you receive them, and you will have them". God always honours His Word!

Circle Books

Circle is a symbol of infinity and unity. It's part of a growing list of imprints, including o-books.net and zero-books.net.

Circle Books aims to publish books in Christian spirituality that are fresh, accessible, and stimulating.

Our books are available in all good English language bookstores worldwide. If you can't find the book on the shelves, then ask your bookstore to order it for you, quoting the ISBN and title. Or, you can order online—all major online retail sites carry our titles.

To see our list of titles, please view www.Circle-Books.com, growing by 80 titles per year.

Authors can learn more about our proposal process by going to our website and clicking on Your Company > Submissions.

We define Christian spirituality as the relationship between the self and its sense of the transcendent or sacred, which issues in literary and artistic expression, community, social activism, and practices. A wide range of disciplines within the field of religious studies can be called upon, including history, narrative studies, philosophy, theology, sociology, and psychology. Interfaith in approach, Circle Books fosters creative dialogue with non-Christian traditions.

And tune into MySpiritRadio.com for our book review radio show, hosted by June-Elleni Laine, where you can listen to authors discussing their books.

MySpiritRadio